CRIMES BY STARLIGHT

COLLECTED POEMS
2009 – 2014

DEAN MEREDITH

ISBN: 978-1-925590-61-6
Published by Vivid Publishing
A division of Fontaine Publishing Group
P.O. Box 948, Fremantle
Western Australia 6959
www.vividpublishing.com.au

Cataloguing-in-Publication data is available from the National Library of Australia

CONTENTS

OUTSIDE OUT

OWED TO LEONARD

PAIR OF SHOES

PANNING FOR GOLD

PEARL IN THE SKY

PERFORMANCE ARTISTE

PINK

PLEASE SIR

POETRY COURT

POLARITY

PROUST

Q & A

QUIETLY SEARCHING

RAW

RESPECTABLE

SEEING ME

SHADOW BOXER

SILLY LITTLE DREAMS

'SMILE HENRY'

SOMETHING ABOUT YOU

SO REAL

SO SHORT

SO WRITE

STICKS & STONES

STRAY CAT CAFÉ

STREET MUSIC

SWEET RAIN

SYMPTOMATIC

TAPPED

TEENAGE GIRLS

TEN PAST FOUR

THAT RABBIT

THE CLOSER YOU GET

THE COLD OLD FOREST

THE CUTEST THING

THE LADY AND ME

THE LETTER

THE PRINCESS AND THE LUNE

1ST NIGHT

I SO STILL & QUIET

LIKE SOFT LITTLE MOUSY

SHE SO QUIRKY

AND LISTENS THROUGH HAIR

HE SO FUNNY

LIKE FRIENDLY GONZO

SHE SO BROWN

AND MIND LIKE RAINBOW

HE WITH TIME

PLAYS WITH MONEY

SHE SO TALL

LIPS LIKE HONEY

SHE SO NICE

AND MELANCHOLY

HE LIKE SALT

SHE SO ERNEST

AND HIM SO PROPER

AND HE LIKE GRAPE

ALL SO CLEVER

23

THEY GAVE ME DAYS

THEY GAVE ME 23

TO LIVE AND BREATHE

AND REALLY SEE

THEY GAVE ME DAYS

THEY GAVE ME 23

DAYS OF CALENDARS

AND CLOCKS

TWENTY-THREE

TWENTY-THREE

AND AFTER ALL

HIS MIRACLES

HE STILL BELIEVED

IN TWENTY-THREE

HAS HE?

SMELLED YOUR FUR?

QUITE POSSIBLY

IF IT WERE ONLY

TWENTY-THREE

BUT IT"S ALL A BIG IF

WHETHER OR NOT

SHE"S TRUE

TWENTY-THREE

I DON"T KNOW

BUT TWENTY-THREE

ONE LAST HURRAH

FOR TWENTY-THREE

ACCUSATIONS FRY

TWO POEMS

THE BEST AND WORST OF ME

I"M NOT PROUD

PREPPY SNOB YOU SAY

NOT GUILTY I SAY

HOMOPHOBE YOU SAY

LIAR I SAY

MISOGYNIST YOU SAY

YOU DON'T KNOW ME

A DARK WIND BLEW

WHAT WAS THAT?

THE WIND SAID

AS IT BREATHED

… DEATH

INTO THE ROOM

AND WEAVED

A WITHERED FOOT

AND LIMPED

CANDLE LIT

… UNHOLY

IN THE GLOOM

IT SAID …

RUSH AWAY

BE GONE

BE GONE

AND SOON

A STORM OF THOUGHTS

THUNDERED ON

AND RAINED ...

OVER THE MOON

OLD DEAD WOOD

CREAKED AND MOANED

GRINDING TEETH ...

THROUGH SKIN AND BONE

BLOOD SPARKS FLEW

FROM RUSTED NAILS

WINDOWS SHRIEKED

THE BANSHEE WAILED

BEAUTIFULLY DONE SON

BEAUTIFULLY DONE

THE DARKNESS ...

WILL HELP YOU SEE

'A' MINOR

MY MELANCHOLY FRIEND

A RESINOUS BOW

THE QUEEN BEE

COVERED IN POLLEN

AND HER DRONES

ALL AROUND HER

THE MAIDEN HAIR

HOW THE HONEY STICKS

HER DOWN BETWEEN HIS LEGS

THE LONG SLOW BUZZ

THE BACK AND FORTH

THE STRINGS

THE NECK

THE BODY

THE SPIKE

AM I TOASTED?

WILL I CRUMBLE?

AND FALL APART?

OR AM I JUST

CRUMBY AND STALE

CHEAP WHITE BREAD

WITH A BROWNISH HUE

EVEN THE CHEESY BITS

ARE A BIT FLAKY

AND THE BUTTER

SPREAD TOO THICK

BAMBI

IT IS NIGHT AND THE JUNGLE LIVES

EXCITED MONKEYS CHATTER

BIRDS CALL AND ANSWER

A FULL MOON COLOURS LEAVES TREES GRASSES - GREEN

A BROWNISH MIST RISES, THICK FROM THE EARTH

A MUSTY SMELL WAFTS THROUGH FERNS PALMS

SPIDER WEBS STRETCH HEAVY WITH INSECTS

THIRSTY MOSQUITOES HANG IN THE HEAT

THE BACKDROP - A VEIL OF BLACK

A DOE-EYED DEER CREEPS CAUTIOUSLY INTO A CLEARING

A CITY OF EYES, LOOK ON, AFRAID TO BLINK

THE DEER MEANDERS, ALONE, LOST

BREATHING SLOWS

HEARTBEATS SYNCHRONIZE

NOISE TAILS OFF

CROSS-HAIRS FOCUS

SILENCE

THEN THE QUICK FLICK OF A SWITCH

AND A GREAT BRIGHT LIGHT MAKES DAY FROM NIGHT

SHOCKED, DAZED

THE LITTLE FAWN FREEZES IN HOT WHITE FEAR

THREE HARD FINGERS SQUEEZE TRIGGERS

RAW INSTINCT SETS IN, THE DEER THINKS TO BOLT

ITS KNEES WOBBLE, AND TREMBLING, IT STUMBLES

SLOWLY FALLING LIKE A FLOATING FEATHER

AND CRUMPLES INTO THE GROUND

THE SOUND OF GUNFIRE ECHOES AROUND AND DIES

A WAILING CRY RINGS OUT

ANOTHER AND ANOTHER

UNTIL A FRENZIED CACOPHONY RAGES FROM THE BOUGHS

AND NOT A HUNTER IS HEARD

AS THEY SILENTLY DRAG THE FRESH LIFELESS FORM

AND THE BLOOD RUNS FREE STILL WARM AS IT FLOWS

OVER GRASS AND LEAVES AND STICKS LIKE PAINT

TO MOSS AND CLAY ON THE SOFT MOIST FLOOR

THEN QUICK AS THEY CAME THEY ARE GONE AGAIN

AND IT IS DARK ONCE MORE

BEAUTIFUL THINGS

I NEED TO LET YOU KNOW

IN CASE YOU"VE FORGOTTEN

OR NEVER REALIZED TO BEGIN WITH

THAT YOU"RE ALL BEAUTIFUL

I"M NOT JUST SAYING IT

I REALLY MEAN IT

LET ME TRY AND EXPLAIN

YOU SEE, EVERY DAY

ON TV AND AT WORK

THERE"S ALL THIS HORROR

SO WHENEVER I GET OUT

AND ESCAPE FROM IT ALL

AND I"M BLESSED WITH TIME

TO PAUSE AND LOOK

SOMETIMES I GET TO REALLY SEE

AND IF I"M VERY LUCKY

I WATCH WITH WONDER

AS EVERYDAY THINGS COME ALIVE

I"VE ALWAYS HAD A SENTIMENTAL STREAK

I BECOME ATTACHED TO THINGS

LIKE MY OLD SECOND-HAND CARS

WITH ALL THEIR PROBLEMS

AND BROKEN BITS

AND PARTS THAT DON"T WORK

AFTER YEARS OF NEGLECT

YEAH, I TALK TO THEM

GIVE THEM GENDERS

NAMES AND PERSONALITIES

AND BEGIN TO LOVE THEM

LIKE FAMILY AND FRIENDS

I GRIEVE WHEN THEY GO

BECAUSE THEY"RE A PART OF ME

AND I NEVER REALLY FORGET THEM

THEN NEWER ONES COME ALONG

AND I FALL FOR THEM TOO

I GIVE THEM ATTENTION

BUT OVER TIME

I START TAKING THEM FOR GRANTED

AND AS I GET OLDER

I REALIZE WHAT I"M DOING

SO I MAKE AN EFFORT

AND FIND TIME FOR THEM

AND THEY"RE GOOD TO ME

AND WE"RE HAPPY TOGETHER

AND WHEN I SIT OUTSIDE

AND THE LIGHT IS JUST RIGHT

THEY APPEAR YOUNG AGAIN

ALL CLEAN AND SHINY

LIKE THE FIRST DAY WE MET

AND WE TOUCH EACH OTHER

IN MY MIND

AND WE SEEM RELAXED

I GUESS THAT"S CONTENTMENT

SO I THANK GOD

AND LOOK TO THE SKY

AND IT"S ALWAYS BEAUTIFUL

EVEN ON THE WORST DAYS

WHEN THE SUN"S UNHAPPY

AND IT SEEMS LIKE

HE"S TRYING TO FRY US ALL

EVEN THEN IF WE"RE HONEST

THE BLUE IS STILL BEAUTIFUL

SO WHEN I LOOK

AT ALL YOU WEEDS AND FLOWERS

I THINK ...

WHAT A MAGNIFICENT GARDEN

FULL OF VARIETY AND COLOUR

AND I THINK ...

HOW LUCKY AM I?

BLACK AND BLUE

WHY IS THE SKY?

SO DARK TONIGHT

LIKE A SHROUD

WAITING TO FALL

ON ALL BELOW

ELMS OF LIME

AND LEMONY GOLD

A LIP RED LIGHT

ALL ALLURING

ON THE CORNER

WHAT"S THAT BLACK?

IS IT BLUE BLACK?

OR THAT NEW BLACK

BLACK ON BLACK

ANYTHING

TO GET HER BACK

BLASTED BULB

DAMNED BRIGHT SPARK LIGHT

CAUGHT ME READING

WHEN I SHOULDN'T BE

SO WHAT DOES IT DO?

GOES AND TURNS OFF ON ME

JUST LIKE THAT

ONE MINUTE ALL WHITE

THE NEXT ALL BLACK

OH THE POWER

BOTTLE BRUSH

BY THE BRISTLING BOTTLE BRUSH

HE LIED TO LAY HIS LOVELY LUSH

AND DRUNKEN DREAMS DID DARKLY DWELL

WITH WEBS OF WORDS IN A WHISKEY WELL

HIS FAIRY-FLOSS HAIR WHITE LIKE COTTON

HER ITCHING SCRATCH NE"ER FORGOTTEN

BUTTERFLY & BEE

HE OFFERED IMPERFECTION

AND SAID IT WAS FOR FREE

I SETTLED FOR DECEPTION

KNEW HE WOULDN"T SEE

HE COULD HAVE IF HE WANTED

BUT HIS EYES WERE JUST FOR ME

I FOUND IT QUITE CONFRONTING

YET CHOSE NOT TO BREAK FREE

THEN HE WENT AND SPOILED IT

I WISHED HE"D LET ME BE

BUT HE WAS SUCH AN IDIOT

AND WORRIED THAT I"D FLEE

HE MAKES PRETTY MUSIC

LIVES IN BIG OLD TREE

THINKS I MAYBE MAGIC

I BUTTERFLY - HIM BEE

CAMEL-TOE

CAMEL-TOE

OH CAMEL-TOE

HOW I LOVE THEE

CAMEL-TOE

THE WAY YOU COME

THE WAY YOU GO

CAMEL-TOE

OH CAMEL-TOE

YOU ONLY SHOW

YOUR OUTER GLOW

WHEN WHAT"S WITHIN

I"D RATHER KNOW

YOUR HILLS AND VALLEYS

DOWN BELOW

YOUR DOUBLE YOU

THAT SEAM YOU SEW

IT"S AS THOUGH

OH CAMEL-TOE

YOU"RE GIVING US

A PRIVATE SHOW

HOW I LOVE THEE

CAMEL-TOE

THE WAY YOU COME

THE WAY YOU GO

CARS HAVE FEELINGS TOO

WE ALL BREAK

IN DIFFERENT WAYS

THE STONE CHIPS

ON OUR PAINTWORK

THE CRACKS

IN OUR LEATHER

THE HOLES

IN OUR RETREADS

THE BENDS

IN OUR BODIES

THE RUST STAINS

SHOWING OUR AGE

LIGHTS AND MIRRORS

SMASH TO PIECES

SOMETIMES

BAD LUCK FOLLOWS

WE CAN BE FIXED

BUT NEVER EXACTLY

AS WE WERE

CHRISTMAS SNACKS

YEAH SO CAVE AND CO

BLED THEIR MENACE

THROUGH MY MEAT GRINDER

BRAIN ON A HOT SALT

RAIN DRIPPING

CLOUD COVERED

LIBERATING LIBATIOUS

BEER SOAKED

PIZZA PERFECT

GARLIC FINGERED

ALMOST SUMMER DAY

BUT I FELT COOL

LOOKED LIKE A

LIQUORED UP HAS-BEEN

THRONE BACK

FROM A BARRED ROOM

PATHETIC ONE HOOKER

DANCE AND I LAND

WITH A BOUNCE

LIKE A FAT KING RAT

ALL BELLY AND WHISKERS

TAIL IN TACT

NOSE POINTED

AND A QUIRKY

LITTLE ALLEY CAT

INVITES ME HOME

TO SHARE HER BISCUITS

SHE HAS ME FOR DINNER

I HAVE HER FOR DESSERT

THEN SHE SHOWS ME

HER SECRET KITTY STASH

AND SHE LOOKS SO CUTE

WITH THOSE GREEN ALMOND EYES

AND HER I'VE GOT IT WALK

AND HER TAIL IN THE AIR

SO I GET DOWN

AND DEVOUR THOSE BONES

SUCKING THE MARROW

LICKING THE BEST BITS

CLEAN AND DRY

THEN WE PAUSE

TO DEVELOP OUR CRAZY SMILES

AND ROLL ON OUR BACKS

AND DRIFT OFF LIKE BATS

AS THOUGH IT ALL WAS A

DREAM OF SORTS

WHERE ROLES GET BLURRED

AND POSITIONS REVERSED

AND IT JUST DON"T MATTER

WHO FOLLOWS OR LEADS

COZ THAT STUFF JUST

GETS IN THE WAY

IT"S ALL ABOUT THE MUSIC

AND ALL ABOUT THE SONG

AND FEELING

THE WORDS

THEY SAY

CONFESSIONS OF A LUNATIC

THE HIGH LIFE

THAT"S THE RIGHT LIFE

THE RIGHT LIFE

FOR ME

IT"S PLEASURE

MIXED WITH PLEASURE

INFINITY

PLUS THREE

MY MIND

IT CRAWLS THE CEILING

AND LOOKS ON DOWN

AT ME

THE BLUR

IS OUT OF FOCUS

NEITHER EYE

CAN SEE

BLINK TWICE

BEHIND THE MIRROR

BLINK TWICE

AND LET IT BE

CRIMES BY STARLIGHT

AND SHE VISITED

LIKE IT WAS OLD TIMES

AND THEY WERE NERVOUS

LIKE IT WAS OLD TIMES

BUT THE KISSES

WERE DEEP

AND UNTROUBLED

AND IT SHOULD HAVE STOPPED THERE

BUT IT HADN'T

AND HIS MISTAKE

WAS HERS

AND THEY WERE CRIMINALS

AND THEY WERE

JUST RIGHT

BUT BROKEN

AND THE MOON

AND ALL THE STARS

WERE JUST RIGHT

BUT BROKEN

AND HE SMILED

LIKE LIFE WOULD NEVER END

AND SHE SMILED

BECAUSE SHE WAS HAPPY

AND LIFE

SEEMED LIKE

DEATH

AGAIN

CROSSING THE LINE

OH THAT"S QUITE A PAIR

OF LEGS YOU HAVE THERE

YOU CROSS THEM SO EASILY

LIKE TWO LIVE WIRES

POSITIVE AND NEGATIVE

SEPARATE BUT CONNECTED

BY A SECRET SOMETHING

SURGING FROM WITHIN

DARK STRANGER

HELLO MISTER

YOU RAGGED OLD THING

ALL RUFFLED FEATHERS

AND BLACK SHARPNESS

MENACING LOOKS

GARBLED CRIES

MISUNDERSTOOD

BUT FASCINATING

CONTINUALLY TAUNTED

BY SMALL MINDS

SHADOW PUPPETS

AGAINST THE SUN

YOU TERRIFY

AND ENTHRAL

WITH YOUR MYSTERY

APPEAR FROM NOWHERE

EYE US THROUGH

AND THEN ...

YOU"RE GONE

DEAR QUEEN

I SHALL SEND

EACH NIGHT AT EIGHT

A LITTLE KISS

TO YOUR RUSTY GATE

FINDING IT LOCKED

AND HIM BEING SMALL

HE WON'T BE ABLE

TO CLIMB YOUR WALL

YOUR LETTER BOX

HIS ONLY HOPE

HIS RESTING PLACE

AN ENVELOPE

DÉJÀ VU

TWO MEN

WALK ALONE

AT THE SAME TIME

BUT YEARS APART

BOTH LOOK

TO THE PAST

FOOTSTEPS SIMILAR

BUT NOT THE SAME

THE SAND KNOWS THEM

AN OLD SIROCCO

PLEADS INDIFFERENCE

JUST BECAUSE IT CAN

AND HISTORY KNOWS

ALWAYS REMEMBERS

IT FELT THE FOOTPRINTS

DEEP WITHIN

ALL SO SERIOUS

LAUGHING

AS THEY GO

DELIVER ME

JUDAS

DELIVER ME

QUICKLY

UNDAMAGED

INTACT

VIA

AMERICAN EXPRESS

TO NEW YORK

TO NEW ROME

OR BEIJING

INFORM BERLIN

INFORM MOSCOW

LONDON, PARIS

NEW DELHI

JERUSALEM

DON"T FORGET

YOUR SHEKELS

OR YOUR

PIECES OF GOLD

DELIVER ME

SO THE FUTURE

MAY BE TOLD

AND TRACK

MY PROGRESS

AS I"M SOLD

RECORD

MY SUMMITS

RECORD

MY FALLS

FORGIVE

MY WEAKNESS

MY

HUMANITY

MY SELFISHNESS

FOR ALL

DELIVER ME

MY

FAITHFUL FRIEND

AND I"LL SEE YOU

IN HIS HALL

DOWN UNDER

DEATH CAME

AS A GARDENER

WITH FORK AND SPADE

HE SMILED AND SEEMED

HAPPY TO SEE ME

WISH I COULD SAY THE SAME

BUT I WAS READY

MY WORK WAS DONE

I"D SOWED MY SEED

AND LIVED TOO LONG

SO WHERE"S THE FIRE?

YOU SEE

I HAD FLAMES IN MIND

OH THAT"S BELOW

HE SAID

SO I SAID

LEAD THE WAY

SO HE DID

AND BEFORE TOO LONG

WE WERE DEEP UNDERGROUND

IN A TORCH LIT TUNNEL

WINDING LIKE A SERPENT

IT TOOK SOME TIME

HE WAS IN A HURRY

I WASN'T

THEN THERE WE WERE

IT WASN'T LIKE I'D IMAGINED

HELL IT WAS HUGE

AND EVERYONE WAS THERE

DREAMING OF HAPPY

WE'RE ALWAYS SORRY

AFTER SHOWING OUR WORST

TO THE ONES WE ADORE

WHO LOVE US THE MOST?

TAKING US BACK

AGAIN AND AGAIN

DESPITE THEIR BEST THOUGHTS

HEARTS BIGGER THAN FOREVER

INNOCENT STRAY KITTENS

FULL OF SOFT HOPE

BLIND AS STREET LIGHTS

SEARCHING FOR STARS

IMPOSSIBLY FAR

FROM HOMELY DRAINS

AND THIN SPIDER FRIENDS

ALL DREAMING OF HAPPY

BUT SETTLING FOR TOMORROW

ONE CRAZY MOON

AFTER ANOTHER

SMILING AT PAIN

THROUGH RAIN SOAKED MUD

FORGIVING THEIR BRUTES

POOR SWEET BROTHERS

OUT TO IMPRESS

THOSE FATHERLY GHOSTS

BLOWING BREATHY FINGERS

SHAKING ONE MORE GAME

LOADED DICE SPINNING

PRAYING LIKE HELLFIRE

FOR HIM AND FOR THEM

ROLLING POINT ON POINT

WITH CRUSHED VELVET SLIDE

UNTIL THE FLAT STOP

OF SKID ROW BONE

AND THEIR LITTLE HEADS

CLOSER THAN A FAMILY

MILK WHITE TOGETHER

PINK TONGUES LAPPING

HUNGRY AS A WEDDING

DANCING JUST FOR FUN

TAKING US BACK

AGAIN AND AGAIN

ERNESTLY DREAMING

HE SHOWS HIS WORST

WHICH ARE A FEW THOUGHTS

AND WORDS

AND SHE

NOT BEING STUPID

SEES THAT

BUT

WHAT DOES SHE THINK?

HE ERNESTS

A MAN

WHO CAN SHOW HIS WORST

AS A WARNING

AS A GUIDE

SHE COULD DO WORSE

HE KNEW THAT TOO

IN A DREAM

THEY CAME TOGETHER

AND IN A DREAM

THEY STAYED

FERAL MOAN

YOU PUT YOUR SCENT ON ME

AND I WAS YOURS

YOU WAIVED YOUR TAIL IN THE AIR

AND SKUNKED ME

YOU SCRAMBLED MY SENSES

LIKE A STEALTH BIMBO

YOU CARPET FUCKED ME

AND BURNED A STAIN

YOU SCREWED ME UP AND IN

LIKE A FLASHING BULB

AND YOUR DEXTROUS FINGERS

FLICKED MY SWITCH

FIREFLIES

I'LL COME

WHEN NO-ONE"S THERE

I'LL COME

WHEN I"M NOT EXPECTED

I'LL DO WHAT"S RIGHT

FOR THE WRONG REASONS

AND WHAT"S WRONG

FOR WHAT I THINK IS RIGHT

I'LL DREAM OF FIREFLIES

CIRCLING IN THE NIGHT

I'LL WONDER

AIMLESSLY

AND WANDER

OUT OF SIGHT

WITH MY FLICKER OF LOVE

BURIED DEEP WITHIN

TO KEEP IT FROM THE WIND

AND IN MY GLOVE

I'LL HOLD ON TIGHT

WITH ALL MY FADING MIGHT

UNTIL INEVITABLY

MY BLOOD STARVED HAND

RELEASES

UNKNOWING

AND I FALL

OVER AND OVER

EVER LOWER

WAITING

FOR AN END

EXPECTING PAIN

BUT FREE

FOR A FEW SECONDS

TO GLIMPSE THE FIREFLIES

ONE MORE TIME

FLOWERS

TODAY I LOOKED FOR FLOWERS

I HAD ROSES IN MIND

BUT ALL I FOUND WERE POPPIES

MY FIRST THOUGHT WAS DEATH

AND THEN REMEMBRANCE

BUT NEXT CAME COURAGE

AND SELF SACRIFICE

AND THE ETERNAL FLAME

AND LOVE AND PEACE

I WANTED TO GIVE YOU A FLOWER

I WANTED TO GIVE YOU A BUNCH

I WANTED TO FILL YOUR CAR

I WANTED TO FILL YOUR LIFE

WITH FLOWERS AND COLOUR AND BEAUTY

THEN I REALISED THAT

GOD HAS ALREADY DONE IT

AND I'M NO GOD

I'M HARDLY EVEN A MAN

AND YOU ARE LOVELIER THAN ANY GARDEN

AND I UNWORTHY TO WEED AROUND YOU

AND YET MY ACID RAIN

CANNOT DAMAGE YOUR INNOCENT PETALS

THEY SEEM TO THRIVE ON IT

AS THOUGH YOU WERE MADE

FOR NUCLEAR WINTER

AS THOUGH MY MUSHROOM CLOUD

WAS JUST A NECESSARY PART

OF YOUR NURTURING NATURE

I FOUND MY FRAGRANT FLOWER

BEAUTY BLESSED AND HEAVEN"S SCENT

GHOSTS OF THE SEA

SHE IS THE MOON

AND HE IS THE SEA

WITHOUT HER HE KNOWS

HE CEASES TO BE

THE SIRENS HE HEARS

WERE ALL SENT BY SHE

THEY ARE JUST FEARS

GHOSTS THAT HE FLEES

WRECKS ON THE BEDS

SHELLS OF HIS SEAS

GOING THINGS

AND WHEN YOU"RE GONE

I"LL HAVE ONE LESS THING

AND UNTIL ALL MY OTHER THINGS GO

I"LL HAVE THEM

AND WHEN THEY"RE ALL GONE

I"LL HAVE NOTHING

WHICH IS AT LEAST A WORD?

GUIDE ME?

WILL YOU GUIDE ME TO THE OTHER SIDE?

WILL YOU WHISPER IN MY EAR?

OR WILL YOU SHOW ME IN MY MIND?

THE SECRET PATH TO TAKE ME CLEAR,

THROUGH THE MINEFIELD, THROUGH THE MIRE,

THROUGH THE CORPSES, THROUGH THE FIRE,

WILL YOU TAKE ME, BE MY GUIDE?

AND NOT FORSAKE ME BECAUSE I LIED,

WILL YOU HIDE ME FROM MY FEARS?

OR WILL YOU DROWN ME IN YOUR TEARS?

WILL YOU FREE ME FROM THEIR SNEERS?

WILL YOU DRAG ME PAST THE PEERS?

OR WILL YOU JUST DECEIVE ME?

AND GO OFF AND LEAVE ME WHERE I LIE,

AND NOT DISTURB MY SLEEPING,

AND JUST IGNORE THEIR WEEPING WHEN I DIE,

AND AFTER WILL YOU COME BACK FOR ME?

EVEN THOUGH I WAS A LIAR,

WILL YOU TAKE ME THROUGH THE WIRE?

WILL YOU REMEMBER HOW I LOVED YOU?

OR WILL YOU THINK OF HOW I DOUBTED AND MISTRUSTED?

WHEN YOU GAVE ME ALL YOU HAD TO GIVE,

WILL YOU WAKE ME FROM MY SLUMBER?

OR WILL YOU DENY ME A REASON TO LIVE?

WILL THAT BE YOUR JUDGEMENT FOR ONE CRIME TOO MANY?

AND IF THERE WERE ANY HOPE OF ACQUITTAL,

WOULD IT BE DASHED BY MY COMMITTAL?

OR WILL I BE TOO CRAZY TO KNOW?

AND IN THE END JUST REFUSE TO GO

HAIKU & SENRYU

A CHURCH

NEXT TO A PUB

WORSHIPPERS GATHER

ANZAC DAY

MARCHERS GET YOUNGER

MEDALS GROW HEAVIER

AUSTRALIAN MADE

EVEN THE DEFECTS

ARE PATRIOTIC

BEES

EARNESTLY HUMMING AWAY

BEES

CREVASSE OF HER ARSE

AND HIDDEN VALLEYS

I MUST EXPLORE

DEATH –

THE WINNER

FINISHES LAST

FAKEBOOK

FALSEBOOK

FARCEBOOK

FOOTPRINTS IN THE SNOW

I FOLLOW COLD AND ALONE

WALKING IN CIRCLES

HE LOOKED TO HIS GOD

WHO LOOKED TO HIS GOD

AND SO ON ...

HOMING PIGEONS

UNDER THE BRIDGE

NOWHERE TO GO

I LEAVE THE SHOP

WITH EVERYTHING

EXCEPT WHAT I NEED

MISSING YOU

I HEAR TAPPING AT WINDOW

HELLO RAIN BIRD

OLD LIBRARY

SO QUIET

AND THOUGHTFUL

POETS

ARE ALIENS

WITH CAMERAS

RELIGIOUSLY

I PARK OUTSIDE THE CHURCH

ONE DAY I"LL GO IN

SHE SPREADS HER FISHNETS

AND IS SATISFIED

HE"S QUITE A CATCH

SUMMER RAIN

DROPLETS GLISTEN

AIR SWEETENS

SUNLIGHT BECKONS

SWIM UP

SWIM UP

THE NEIGHBOURS

PUTTING RUBBISH IN MY BIN

SHOULD I BE ENVIOUS

TWITS TWEETING

OH FUCK –

ALLITERATION

WANK WORDS -

STEEP LEARNING CURVE

ABSOLUTELY

WAR CRIMES

PROPAGANDA

WAR IS CRIME

WILLY WAG TAIL

TWISTS IN TIME

WITH SPRINKLER

WITHOUT KNOWING

I HIDE THE KEYS

FROM MYSELF

WRAPPED IN CREPE PAPER

HER LAST CHRISTMAS PRESENT

CRADLED AS SHE SLEEPS

HAPPY ENDINGS

THERE GO THOSE HAPPY ENDINGS

THERE THEY GO

ALL THOSE LOVELY HAPPY ENDINGS

THERE THEY GO

NO MORE LOVELY HAPPY ENDINGS

ANYMORE

THEY'VE ALL GONE AWAY

GOODBYE MY LOVELY HAPPY ENDINGS

HOW I LOVED YOU FOR A WHILE

I'LL THINK ABOUT YOU MY HAPPY ENDINGS

I'LL THINK ABOUT YOU FOR A WHILE

GOODBYE GOODBYE MY HAPPY ENDINGS

I'LL THINK ABOUT YOU FOR A WHILE

GOODBYE GOODBYE MY HAPPY ENDINGS

GOODBYE I LOVED YOU FOR A WHILE

I'LL CALL YOU LATER HAPPY ENDINGS

I'LL SEE YOU ,ROUND IN A WHILE

HARD SHOE

MM ...

THAT SOUND ...

OF HER LONG ... SLOW

... HIGH HEEL TOE

ON THE HARD WOOD FLOOR

ON THE OTHER SIDE

OF THE THIN GREEN WALL

WITH THE SMOKY WINDOW

IN THE SMALL DARK ROOM

WITH THE LOCK ON THE DOOR

NEXT TO ALL THE OTHER

SMALL DARK ROOMS

WITH THIN GREEN WALLS

AND LOCKS ON THE DOORS

AND SMOKY WINDOWS

ALL WITH VIEWS TO THE STAGE

WITH HER AND THOSE SHOES

AT THE CENTRE OF ATTENTION

FROM THE WINDOWS OF THE ROOMS

WITH THE LOCKS ON THE DOORS

AND THE THUMP OF THE MUSIC

AND THE PUMP OF HER SHOES

AS SHE STRUTS AROUND

ON THE HARD WOOD FLOOR

WITH HER LONG ... SLOW

... HIGH HEEL TOE

AND THE COINS IN THE SLOTS

KNOW WHERE TO GO

AND SHE LOOKS LIKE A MOVIE

AND SHE SOUNDS LIKE A STAR

THEN SHE STOPS AT YOUR WINDOW

PUTS HER FOOT IN THE AIR

RESTS A HEEL ON YOUR WALL

AND YOU CAN'T HELP BUT STARE

AND SHE LIKES HOW YOU LOOK

AND HER EYES SAY IT ALL

AND YOU COME LIKE A SAILOR

AND SHE SMILES COZ SHE KNOWS

AND YOUR WINDOW FOGS UP

AND YOUR CURTAIN IS CLOSED

AND ALL YOU CAN HEAR IS

THE SOUND OF THOSE SHOES

AND HER LONG ... SLOW

... HIGH HEEL TOE

ON THE HARD WOOD FLOOR

ALL SATISFIED ...

AS SHE GOES

HATE

CARRIED

HARD HEAVY

LONG BLACK SACK

WHITE NYLON NOOSE

DIGS IN

HURTS

HUNG TIGHT

GRIP RELAXES

RELEASES

DUMB THUD

USELESS CORPSE

UNFEELING

STARING BACK

BLINDLY

PAIN GOES

GRIMACE FOLLOWS

FINGERS FLEX

PINK SORROW

MARKS FADE

BRUTE BAG DRAGGED

SOMEWHERE ELSE

A CORNER

PROPPED UP PROUD

COLD WALL WITNESS

ALONE FOR NOW

UNTIL THE RETURN

BASTARD SMIRKING

TORN MOUTH

CAVITY EYES

HUNCHED DARKLY

MADLY TWISTED

VICTIMS" SHUFFLE

HAUNTING SHADOW

AFRAID TO GO

HELLO JACKIE O

DON"T BE SO HARD

YOU DO IT TOO

WITH BLACK BEATING SHIRT

AND HAIRY DARK HUE

DON"T MOCK HER PARADE

HER SELF-ESTEEM FAIR

WITHOUT HER YOU"RE NOTHING

NO-ONE, NOWHERE

ALLOW HER A MOMENT

AND HELP HER TO DARE

TO FEEL LIKE SOMEONE

THAT REALLY IS THERE

SHE"LL WEAR WHAT SHE WANTS

AND DO AS SHE PLEASE

YOU HAVE NO RIGHT

TO SNICKER OR TEASE

FOR SHE IS A LADY

AND SHE IS THE SEA

YOU ARE BUT SAND

THAT SHE HAS LET BE

HEMLOCK AND HONEY

I'VE DONE SO MANY DEALS

WITH ALL TYPES OF DEVILS

MOST OF THEM SAINTLY

IN SOME KINDLY WAY

FUNNY HOW THINGS

AREN'T QUITE AS THEY SEEM

WE SIP FROM THOSE CUPS

AND SOMETIMES THE POISON

TASTES SWEETER

THAN ANY NECTAR OF GODS

HERR DOKTOR

MY SYMPTOMS

REAL AND IMAGINED

YOU ARE LIBERATOR

AND ACCOMPLICE

I HAVE HEARD

YOUR COLLEAGUE

WHEN HE SAID

ANYTHING YOU WANT

AND THEN I SAW

HIS HANDS SHAKE

POOR DEAR THING

AND HIS WIFE

COVERING FOR HIM

POOR DEAR THING

AND I THE PATIENT

DYING EVERY DAY

REAL AND IMAGINED

HIDE AND SEEK

HERE I AM

IN MY MIND

AGAIN

STILL

AND YOU"RE HERE

WITH ME

AGAIN

STILL

I"M HIDING

FROM YOU

WITH YOU

AGAIN

STILL

COUNT TO TEN

MAYBE ELEVEN

ONE MORE MINUTE

WITH YOU

AGAIN

STILL

DID YOU FIND ME?

I"M A GOOD HIDER

NOT AS GOOD AS YOU

I CAN'T FIND YOU

AGAIN

STILL

HOOKED

I'VE BEEN LURKING DOWN HERE DEEP,

IN COLD CONSTANT NIGHT,

SOMETIMES I SWIM UP,

AND SPY THE SURFACE SHAPES,

THEIR SILHOUETTES BENEATH THE LIGHT,

I DON'T GET TOO CLOSE,

I HEED THE WARNINGS,

OF THE OLD AND GONE,

AND TALES OF TERROR,

OF MONSTERS FROM LAND,

BUT WHEN I SAW THAT SHINING DANCING HOOK,

IT WAS ALL I COULD SEE,

AND A STRANGE HYPNOTIC HUNGER,

HAD ITS WAY WITH ME,

I GOBBLED YOUR PEARL - SHELL AND ALL,

IN ONE ALMIGHTY PIERCING BITE,

AND DARTING PAIN THROUGH BLEEDING GUM,

SOON REPLACED MY DREAMY DELIGHT,

AS QUICK AS ALL MY WITS AWOKE,

I DOVE AND DOVE WITH NO LOOK BACK,

AND SWAM AND SWAM,

AND FELT THE TEARING STEEL ON MOUTH,

AND PULL OF LINE SO LONG UNENDING,

BARB IN FLESH WITH TIGHTNESS BENDING,

GILLS ALL GASPING OPEN GAPING,

FINS SO SORE FROM MAD DESCENDING,

CHEEK ALL SLICED FROM CONSTANT PULLING,

I FEEL MY STRUGGLE SLOWLY ENDING,

NERVOUS BLOODY PULSES SENDING,

SLIPPING BACK I THINK NOT KNOWING,

DRAGGING DRIFTING REDNESS FLOWING,

SUDDEN SURGES SEND ME THRASHING,

LASHING OUT AT FEARS OF GOING,

OFF TO DIE AND THEN BE EATEN,

TENDER MERCILESSLY BEATEN,

HUNG UP HIGH WITH EYES ALL POPPING,

DRIPPING DRY IN WIND SAILS FLAPPING,

PECKING BIRDS SQUAWKING CLAPPING,

LICKING BEAKS READY FOR FEASTING,

HUMANS HURRIEDLY STEER RETURNING,

TO SILENT TOWNS SOFTLY SLEEPING,

BUT I"M AWAKE AND STILL IN WATER,

WHILE YOU"RE CELEBRATING LAUGHING,

ONE LAST SURGE I"M NOT DONE YET,

WITH ALL THE CRAZY STRENGTH LEFT IN ME,

I ZIP AND ZING LIKE LIQUID LIGHTNING,

SNAPPING LINE TOO TAUGHT FROM TIGHTENING,

I"M FREE I"M FREE AND FLEEING SWIFTLY,

FEELING LIGHTNESS NOW UPON ME,

I WEAR MY BODY PIERCING PROUDLY,

AND PRAY ONE DAY TO FIND YOU PADDLING,

SO I MAY TURN THE TIDE MY CAPTOR,

AND TEAR THE PAGE FROM YOUR LAST CHAPTER.

HOORAY FOR MILK!

FOR STANDING UP TO PLATE

AND HIS CRONIES -

PLAIN AND PEANUT BUTTER

THEN ALONG CAME MARMALADE

HOTEL

RED DRESS

SPOTLIGHT

HAIR BLACK

SKIN WHITE

COLD KEYS

TOUCH LIGHT

RED HAIR

FIRE LIGHT

BLACK TIE

SHIRT WHITE

NEW NEWS

UPTIGHT

RED CHAIR

HOT LIGHT

BOOKSHELF

UPRIGHT

WINDOW

SHUT TIGHT

RED DOOR

COOL NIGHT

RAINBOW

STREETLIGHT

GOLD DUST

TOO BRIGHT

HOW TO SPOT A PERVERT

WE ARE MASTERS AND MISTRESSES OF DISGUISE, AND MOST ADEPT AT LOOKING NORMAL.

WE HAVE EXCELLENT EYESIGHT, MIGHT STILL WEAR GLASSES, AND MAY OR MAY NOT HAVE MENTALLY UNDRESSED YOU, WHILE LOOKING YOU STRAIGHT IN THE EYES AND WITHOUT YOU KNOWING.

WE ARE HIGHLY FASHION CONSCIOUS, AND DRESS SO BADLY WE NEITHER MAKE STATEMENTS NOR TRY TO BE AHEAD OF OUR TIME.

WE ARE EXPERTS IN THE BEDROOM; HOWEVER THIS ONLY APPLIES TO THE SUBTLE MOVING AND POSITIONING OF FURNITURE.

WE ARE GREAT LOVERS OF FOOD AND CAN COOK, EAT AND DRINK, ALL IN THE ONE KITCHEN; BUT WE ARE NOT GASTRONOMES - THAT WOULD BE SHOWING OFF.

WE PREFER OUR OWN CARS TO BUSES AND TRAINS. IN OUR OWN CARS WE CAN PICK OUR NOSES IN PRIVATE.

WE KNOW ABOUT ART, INCLUDING FILMS, MUSIC AND PAINTING, BUT WE DON'T ALWAYS GET IT.

WE ARE INHERENTLY LAZY CREATURES, AND PREFER WATCHING TV AND SLEEPING TO ANYTHING ELSE.

WE LIKE LIBRARIES, BECAUSE THE BOOKS ARE USUALLY QUIET.

WE DETEST PUBLIC TOILETS - THEY ARE IMPOSSIBLE TO FIND AND INEVITABLY BY THE TIME WE GET THERE, WE HAVE A NEW TRAUMATIC EXPERIENCE TO SHARE WITH OUR PSYCHOLOGISTS.

WE HAVE FAMILIES AND FRIENDS WHO WE DON"T REALLY
KNOW AND WHO DON"T REALLY KNOW US, AND THAT"S
PROBABLY JUST AS WELL.

WE ARE INCREDIBLY SHALLOW PEOPLE WITH DEEP
THOUGHTS, STRONG HEARTS AND WEAK MINDS.

WE ARE NATURAL COWARDS WHO GO PLACES WE SHOULDN"T
AND FEEL MORE THAN WE SHOULD.

WE ARE NOT NICE, BUT THOSE CLOSEST TO US THINK WE
ARE. FOOLS – AT LEAST WE SHARE THAT IN COMMON.

WE AIM TO BE STRANGE, BUT NOT DIFFERENT, AND OFTEN
JUST SETTLE FOR WEIRD.

WE ARE EVERYBODY AND WE ARE NOBODY, EXCEPT FOR
THOSE TIMES WHEN WE"RE SOMEBODY IN BETWEEN.

WE ARE ACTUALLY IMPOSSIBLE TO FIND, UNLESS YOU"RE ONE
OF US TOO.

I'D LIKE TO MEET YOUR DRAGON

I"D LIKE TO MEET YOUR DRAGON

THE ONE WHO GUARDS YOUR CAVE

I"D PROMISE NOT TO ENTER

I,,D PROMISE TO BEHAVE

I"D TRY TO SEE HIS COLOURS

AND MAYBE SHOW HIM MINE

HOPEFULLY HE"LL DISCOVER

I"M HARMLESS AND I"M FINE

WE"LL LEARN TO TRUST EACH OTHER

AND NEVER CROSS THE LINE

I"D DO THAT FREE AND WILLINGLY

WITHOUT MY SHIELD OR SWORD

KNOWING HE COULD BE KILLING ME

IF I SOUGHT THE WRONG REWARD

YOUR CAVE IS SAFE I WON"T GO IN

MY QUEST IS PURE AND TRUE

NOTHING TO DO WITH PERFECT SKIN

EVERYTHING TO DO WITH YOU

YOUR TREASURES RADIATE AND SHINE

FOR ALL THE WORLD TO SEE

THAT"S THE ONLY WISH OF MINE

A GOLDEN GLIMPSE OF THEE

IF I WERE A GAMBLER

I"D BET

YOU HAVE PEOPLE

FALLING IN LOVE WITH YOU

ALL THE TIME

I"D BET

YOU"RE FLATTERED AND

LET THEM DOWN GENTLY

WHEN YOU CAN

I"D BET

YOU LOVE WILDLY

WITH EVERYTHING YOU HAVE

NOT KNOWING WHY

I"D BET

YOU LEAVE THEM

AND THEY LEAVE YOU

WITHOUT GOOD REASON

I'D BET

SO MANY TIMES

BECAUSE OF YOUR BEAUTY

YOU'VE MISSED CONNECTIONS

I'D BET

THAT STRONG IMAGE

AND AIR OF CONFIDENCE

HIDES YOUR FEARS

I'D BET

WHEN YOU'RE ALONE

YOU LIKE TO CRY

OVER LOST DREAMS

AND I'D BET

ONE FINE DAY

YOU WILL BE GREAT

IN SOME WAY

IN AND OUT

NEEDLE GOES IN

BLOOD COMES OUT

HIT GOES IN

PAIN COMES OUT

RUSH COMES IN

TIDE GOES OUT

DAYS COME IN

NIGHTS GO OUT

LOVE WALKS IN

HATE CRAWLS OUT

HATE CRAWLS IN

LOVE WALKS OUT

THIRST CREEPS IN

HUNGER GOES OUT

WORST CREEPS IN

BEST GOES OUT

CASH COMES IN

CASH GOES OUT

BILLS PILE UP

STASH RUNS OUT

USERS LOB IN

DEALERS SELL OUT

FAMILY CLIMBS IN

CLOCK CHIMES OUT

NEEDLE GOES IN

BLOOD COMES OUT

HIT GOES IN

PAIN COMES OUT

RUSH COMES IN

TIDE GOES OUT

DAYS COME IN

NIGHTS GO OUT

DREAMS FLY IN

DREAMS FLY OUT

DEBTS ADD UP

TIME RUNS OUT

COLLECTORS COME IN

GUNS COME OUT

BULLETS GO IN

BLOOD RUNS OUT

COLD CREEPS IN

WARMTH SEEPS OUT

FEAR SETS IN

LIGHTS GO OUT

AIR COMES IN

BREATH GOES OUT

DEATH COMES IN

SOUL GETS OUT

NEEDLE GOES IN

BLOOD COMES OUT

HIT GOES IN

PAIN COMES OUT

RUSH COMES IN

TIDE GOES OUT

DAYS COME IN

NIGHTS GO OUT

IN BETWEEN

SHE WAS EVERYTHING

AND I WAS NOTHING

AND HER FRIEND

IN BETWEEN

MY HEART SO RIGHT

MY HEAD SO WRONG

AND SIGNS OF TRUTH

FLASHED BY UNSEEN

SUCH WERE THE SIGHTS

THE SOUNDS THE DREAMS

THE RIGHTS THE WRONGS

THE IN BETWEENS

SHE CAME SHE WENT

OR SO IT SEEMED

THE LIES THE TRUTH

THE IN BETWEENS

THE BIRTH THE DEATH

THE IN BETWEEN

SO WEAK SO STRONG

SO IN BETWEEN

SO MANY WAYS

TO LIVE TO DIE

SO FEW DAYS

SO FEW NIGHTS

TO WONDER WHY

TO BE THE DARK

TO BE THE LIGHT

AND ALL THE COLOURS

IN BETWEEN

INDELIBLE

I FELT YOUR BONES

THE DAY THE TRAIN CRUSHED THEM

A COUPLE OF BUMPS IN TIME

THEN PARALYSED SILENCE

AND MY ITINERANT MIND

JUST COULD NOT LEAVE THE SCENE

IN HER GARDEN

THAT NIGHT

SHE TOOK THEM ALL IN

A SHAMBLE OF STRANGERS

AND SHONE THEM A GARDEN

THE OLD WARNED OF DOUBT

BUT LIED

THE YOUNG SHOWED VEINS

PULSING WITH TRUTH

AS HER FRIEND SHARED HER BOSOM

SHE THE ENCHANTRESS

COLLECTED THEIR SOULS

THE SPEAKER STROKED THROUGH

HIS FATHER"S THICK ETHER

AND HER GOLDEN BOY

PLUCKED HIS HARP FULL OF HOPE

HIS SOFT FURRY FRIEND

PURRING ALONG

THE GHOST OF OTHELLO

BURNED LIKE A CAESAR

AND TWO SONS OF MADNESS

CONFUSED EGOS WITH HALOS

WHILE LOST MAGDALENES

SANG SAD DISTANT DIRGES

BY THE FADING LIGHT

OF KAFKA

IN HOBOKEN

THEY"D BEEN POKIN"

ROUN" HOBOKEN

HOPIN" FOR

SOME HILLBILLY GRASS

THE LOCALS JOKIN"
IN HOBOKEN
„BOUT THEM CHOKIN"
AN" FALLIN" ON THEIR ASS

FEW WORDS WERE SPOKEN
IN HOBOKEN
AN" THEY WERE TOKIN"
ON FINE HILLBILLY GRASS

THEN THEY WERE CHOKIN"
IN HOBOKEN
FLOATIN"
OFF THEIR WHITE LILLY ASS

THE LOCALS JOKIN"
IN HOBOKEN
„BOUT THEM SMOKIN"
AN" CHOKIN" ON THEIR GRASS

THEIR DROUGHT WAS BROKIN"

IN HOBOKEN

WITH RAIN SOAKIN"

AN" RUNNIN" DOWN THE GLASS

COZ THEY WERE SMOKIN"

IN HOBOKEN

AN" THEY WERE TOKIN"

ON FINE HILLBILLY GRASS

ALL WERE JOKIN"

IN HOBOKEN

„BOUT THE CHOKIN"

AN" FLOATIN" OFF THEIR ASS

THEY WERE SMOKIN"

IN HOBOKEN

AN" TOKIN"

ON HILLBILLY GRASS

YEAH THEY WERE SMOKIN"

IN HOBOKEN

TOKIN"

ON FINE HILLBILLY GRASS

IN MEMORY OF LOST WORDS

HONESTY RENDERS MEMORY POOR

WORDS THEY FLEE SO EASILY

AS IF THROUGH EVER OPEN DOOR

WICKED WINDS WILL THEM FREE

BUT THEY"RE MINE MADE BY ME

WITHOUT MY MIND THEY"D NOT EXIST

MY INNER EYE GAVE LIFE TO THEE

SILENTLY THEY SINK INTO THE MIST

SHADOWS LEFT BY SUN THEN MOON

ALONE TO FIND AND FEEL THEIR WAY

ORPHANED FROM MY WEEPING WOMB

NOT KNOWING WHETHER NIGHT OR DAY

GO MY CHILDREN AND SEEK THE LIGHT

TRUTH WILL GUIDE TO WHERE IT"S BRIGHT

IN MY MIND

IN MY MIND

THOUGHTS WERE FALLING

IN MY MIND

THEY FELT THE SKY

IN MY MIND

WORDS WERE WEEPING

IN MY MIND

THEY SAID GOODBYE

LAST WISHES

DO NOT BURY ME

I FEAR THE SLITHERING WORMS

LAY ME ON A BED OF HOT COALS

AND BURN ME WELL

SCATTER MY ASHES

IN A GARDEN BY THE SEA

COME VISIT WHEN YOU CAN

AND REMEMBER ME

LITTLE LAMB

I AM WOLF

IN SHEPHERD"S CLOTHING

I SEE EWE

LITTLE LAMB

MY LONG TONGUE

DRIPS ...

WITH ANTICIPATION

DIAMONDS FOR EWE

JUST ONE TASTE

AND LICK OF FLEECE

FEEL MY ROUGH

ON YOUR SOFT

PINK WHITE SKIN

MY PLAN ...

TO DE-FLOCK

AND CHASE EWE

INTO SUBMISSION

THROUGH BLOOD RED EYES

WITH EARS PRICKED

I LUST & LISTEN

BENEATH MY PANTING

YOUR LITTLE HEART BLEATS

AND FOR ONE MAD SECOND

EWE IS MINE

I SHOW MERCY

BUT FEAR

TAKES EWE FROM ME

FLEEING FAST

EWE SCAMPERS AWAY

DON'T LOOK BACK

IN CASE EWE STUMBLES

AND IF EWE DO

WILL ONLY SEE

I DO NOT FOLLOW

I MERELY STAY

WHERE I AM

ENTRANCED ...

BY EWE

LOSING MY RHYME

A SENSE OF HUMOUR

WHAT RHYMES WITH THAT?

CANCER!

A DIGNIFIED DEATH

WHAT RHYMES WITH THAT?

BLOW-JOB!

WORTHLESS WASTED LIFE

WHAT RHYMES WITH THAT?

HARLOTS AND TROUBLE

THAT"S WHAT!

AND THEN …

HOW ABOUT WHORES IN HEAVEN?

WHAT OF THEM?

WELL ABOUT BEATING THEM

ARE YOU REFERRING TO VIOLENCE?

NO I"M TALKING ABOUT

GETTING THERE FIRST

OH!

IT"S NOT A RACE YOU KNOW

THEN WHY IS IT CALLED

THE HUMAN RACE

I DON'T KNOW

BUT YOU"RE EDUCATED

YOU"RE SUPPOSED TO KNOW

EVERYTHING!

WHAT I DO KNOW IS

I'VE LOST MY RHYME

AND MY REASON

DAMN YOU!

NOW WHERE WAS I?

WHO WAS I?

ANOTHER TIME!

OH YES – HEAVEN

WHAT RHYMES WITH THAT?

STALE BREAD OR

A CROOKED NUMBER

TAKE YOUR PICK

I"LL HAVE THE LATTER PLEASE

NUMEROLOGY YOU KNOW

INDEED ...

AND THEN …

WHAT RHYMES WITH BOREDOM?

NOTHING!

LOVE & LUST

ON A HAZY NIGHT WITH HALF A MOON

RUNNING LATE BUT STILL TOO SOON

HER NECTAR SMOOTH, GOLD AND SWEET

PICTURE PERFECT AND SOUL COMPLETE

MUSIC SOFT AND THOUGHTS SET FREE

CURLING SMOKE AND HEARTS THAT SEE

SILKEN TOUCH AND SEDUCTIVE LOOK

WANTING HER OPEN LIKE A BOOK

GENTLE KISSES, CHEEKS AND LIPS

HANDS EXPLORING CURVES AND HIPS

PASSIONS MOUNTING WITH DESIRE

TONGUES TASTING LICKS OF FIRE

SEEING BEAUTY, FEELING MORE

NO IDEA WHAT"S IN-STORE

PRESS AND RUB, JEANS EXPAND

ZIPPER DOWN, ENTER HAND

KNOWING EYES AND WICKED GRIN

SENSUAL MOUTH MADE FOR SIN

SLIPPERY, SLIDING, WARM AND WET

TOO MUCH PLEASURE TO EVER FORGET

SHE TOOK HIM ALL AND ATE IT UP

WOULDN"T ALLOW A DRINK FROM HER CUP

HE WRITHED AND THROBBED, READY TO BURST

NEEDING SO BADLY TO QUENCH HER THIRST

BOTH IN TUNE, BOTH IN BEAT

WANTING JAZZ AND STEAMY HEAT

FLAWLESS FRENCH AND SULTRY HAIR

LOVE AND LUST, WHAT A PAIR

LOVELY THINGS

HALF PAST SEVEN

AND ALREADY DRUNK

I AM WHAT I AM

HE THOUGHT

STEPPING OUT

AND IN

TO SEEMING

BLISS

GIVE US A HUG

LOVELY THING

I"LL STOP SHORT

AT A KISS

MANIFESTO FOR A NICE LIFE

SMOKE THE ROACH

RIGHT TO THE END

BURN YOUR FINGERS

A LITTLE

THINK SOMETIMES

OF THE LONG RUN

BUT LAUGH NOW

WHENEVER YOU CAN

DRINK PLENTY OF RED

EVEN WHEN YOU REALISE

YOU"LL HAVE TO PAY FOR IT

ONE WAY OR ANOTHER

BREAK A FEW

LESS IMPORTANT RULES

BUT KNOW EXACTLY

WHAT YOU"RE DOING

EAT WELL OFTEN

IF YOU CAN AFFORD TO

BUT DON'T MAKE A LIVING

OUT OF IT

WATCH LEAVES DANCE

WRITE CRAZY THOUGHTS

TALK TO ANIMALS AND

HUMANS IF YOU MUST

SLEEP WITH AT LEAST

ONE LIGHT ON AND

A SHARP KNIFE

CLOSE BY

MAYBE

MAYBE SHE"S ALL I"M NOT?

MAYBE SHE"S ALL I CAN BE?

MAYBE SHE"S HER AND

MAYBE SHE"S ME?

ME BEING ME

THIS IS ME

NOT TRYING TO BE

ANYTHING I"M NOT

NO FANCY CLOTHES

NO SINGLE RED ROSE

JUST A HAMBURGER

WITH CHIPS

AND THE LOT

TODAY

I DON"T KNOW WHY

I"M ON ONE OF THOSE

NATURAL HIGHS

I GET

FROM TIME TO TIME

NO ARTIFICIAL JOY

NO DEEP GLASS OF WINE

JUST MY MUSIC AND ME

AND THE AIR THAT I BREATHE

AND MY SUN

WHO NEVER FAILS TO SHINE

METAPSYCHOSIS

THE GRUB EMERGES

SLOWLY

STRUGGLING

WITH WINGS

OF SOME SORT

THE GOO DRIES

A FLAME BECKONS

LIKE A BELLY DANCER

HER NAME IS FATE

MY MAGIC CARPET CIRCLES

EYES FIXED FIRMLY

ON THE PRIZE

CLOSER

CLOSER STILL

HER FLAMES

BREATHE ME IN

AH...

PARADISE!

MOUNT ME

I GET SO HOT

THEN I COOL

I SLEEP & ERUPT

I SPEW ASH

RUMBLE & GRUMBLE

WHERE"S MY VIRGIN?

I BURN DEEP

WITHIN MY MOLTEN CORE

I"M HIGH & I"M LOW

I"M EVERYTHING IN BETWEEN

I"M BEAUTY & I"M HORROR

WHERE"S MY VIRGIN?

I SMOKE & BLEED

I"M OLD & I"LL DIE

I"M MY OWN GRAVE

ONE DAY I"LL BE A GIANT LAKE

I AM YOUR VOLCANO

WILL YOU BE MY VIRGIN?

MY ANGEL

IF SHE"S AN ANGEL

THEN SHE CAN"T STAY TOO LONG

SHE HAS TO GO BACK

WITH A BODY

AND NOT JUST ANYBODY

IF SHE"S MY ANGEL

THEN IT"S MY BODY

THAT"S WHY SHE"S KILLING ME

IT"S NOTHING PERSONAL

SHE"S JUST DOING HER JOB

MY BROTHER THE POET

AND THE WATERS HE WALKED ON

WERE PUDDLES

AND THE BEST HE COULD DO

WAS TURN WINE INTO PISS

AND HIS LOAVES AND FISHES

WERE FROM THE SUPERMARKET

ON SPECIAL

AND HIS THREE WISE MEN

WERE A DRUNK, A THIEF

AND A MURDERER

AND HIS DISCIPLES

WERE SYCOPHANTS

AND HIS CROSS

WAS A CORKSCREW

AND HIS ROCK WAS ROLLED

BY SOMEONE ELSE

BECAUSE HE WAS TOO LAZY

AND HIS RESURRECTION

WAS ONLY IN HIS MIND

WHEN HE GOT HIGH

AND HE WAS ANOTHER NARCISSIST

AND HE WAS JUST LIKE ME

AND HE WAS NOTHING LIKE ME

NO COMPLAINTS HERE

SHE SHINES HER LIGHT

UNEXPECTEDLY

I AM EMBARRASSED

HUMILIATED

AGAIN

BUT HOW CAN I COMPLAIN

AT SUCH BEAUTY

WHEN SHE SHOWS EVERYTHING

AND MY NOTHINGNESS

THANKYOU

NOTHING

HE SAT AND STARED

AND THOUGHT OF NOTHING

EYES ALL SEARCHING

SEEING NOTHING

BLINDLY BLINKING

THINKING NOTHING

WORDS AND PAPERS POISED

FOR ANYTHING

INTO SPACE HE SURELY DRIFTED

FLOATING DREAMING WAITING

NOTHING

HEARING SQUEAKING

THAT WAS SOMETHING

SOMEONE SCRIBBLING

WHILE HE RUSTED

BUT IT WAS NOTHING

WHITEBOARD BLANK

ERASED AND DUSTED

NOT THAT DRUNK

I'M NOT THAT DRUNK

I'M NOT THAT DRUNK

I'M NOT THAT DRUNK

THE AIR SEEMS SOLID

IT"S BACK TO FRONT

THE AIR SEEMS SOLID

GOT ALL THIS JUNK

BUT NOT YOUR FOREHEAD

GOT ALL THIS JUNK

THE AIR SEEMS SOLID

TWO CARS OUT FRONT

BUT NOT YOUR FOREHEAD

I'M OUT TO LUNCH

THE FOOD IS HORRID

I'M OUT TO LUNCH

THE FOOD IS HORRID

I SAW THE PUNCH

I SAW IT COMING

I DIDN'T FLINCH

I SAW IT COMING

I'M NOT THAT DRUNK

NOT THE ONE

I'M THE ONE

YOUR MOTHERS WARNED YOU ABOUT

THE ONE THEY LOVED

BEFORE THE ONE WHO WOULD STAY

I'M THE ONE

YOUR FRIENDS SAY

IS NO GOOD FOR YOU

BUT MIGHT BE OK FOR THEM

I'M THE ONE

WITH ALL THE PROBLEMS

MAYBE EVEN MORE

THAN YOU

I'M THE ONE

WHO WOULD RIDE A WHITE HORSE

AND SAVE YOU

IF I WEREN"T ALLERGIC

I'M THE ONE

WHO MIGHT COMMIT

ALL KINDS OF CRIMES

EXCEPT ADULTERY

I'M THE ONE

WHO TAKES MY MEDICINE

IN REGULAR SMALL DOSES

BUT IS NEVER CURED

I'M THE ONE

WHO IS NOT THE ONE

BUT JUST ONE OF MANY

AND HAPPY TO BE NO-ONE

I"M THE ONE

WITH SOMETHING TO SAY

AND NOWHERE TO SAY IT

BUT I DO ANYWAY

ODE TO A DIRTY OLD MAN

BUKOWSKI

SAT AND READ POETRY

HE ALSO SAT

WHEN HE WROTE IT

HE WAS NEVER YOUNG

BUKOWSKI

HE HIT LIFE HARD

LIKE HIS FATHER"S BELTINGS

WITH GERMAN EFFICIENCY

AND THE LUST

OF A WILD BARBARIAN

BUKOWSKI

NOT LIKE HEMINGWAY

AND HIS BOORISH

MACHO BULLSHIT

NOR RUMSFELD WHO

ALSO STOOD AT HIS DESK

ADDING HIS NEO-CON SHEKELS

NO

HANK WAS HIS OWN MAN

HE CALLED A FUCK A FUCK

AND A PHONY A PHONY

HE LOOKED A MESS BUT

HIS CONSCIENCE WAS NEAT

I COULD BE WRONG

I DIDN"T KNOW HIM

HELL HIS WORDS ONLY

GAVE ME A GLIMPSE

BUT WHAT I SAW WAS

GOODNESS AND HONOUR

THAT BEAUTIFUL UGLY MAN

FILLED WITH RAW HONESTY

UNAFRAID TO BLEED

FROM HIS GUTS FREE

DOWN BUT NEVER OUT

BUKOWSKI

ODE TO A GIRL WITH PERFECT LIPS

HALF A KISS FROM THOSE FULL LIPS

WHY DID I HAVE TO GO?

BECAUSE IT WAS LATE

AND THE MORNING SUN

WAS UP AND WAITING

I COULDN'T WORK

I COULDN'T THINK

MY MIND WAS YOURS

DEVELOPING PHOTOS

IN DARK RED LIGHT

SECRETLY IN MY ROOM

WHEN I SAW YOU NEXT

IN THE BAR ALONE

YOU IGNORED ME SO WELL

IT HURT BUT I LIKED IT

NOT KNOWING WHY

BUT IT SEEMED RIGHT

THEN THE NEXT TIME

YOU WERE FINE AGAIN

CLEAR SKINNED EYES BRIGHT

SMILE LIKE A DREAM

AND HALF A KISS

FROM THOSE FULL LIPS

OH YES

HALF A KISS

AND THOSE FULL LIPS

OH SYLVIA

IF ONLY YOU KNEW

PERHAPS YOU DO

HOW MUCH I FEEL

FOR YOU

IT"S TRUE

YOU LEFT TOO SOON

BUT LEFT A CLUE

OR TWO

YOU LEFT A FEW

IT"S JUST SO SAD

BUT NOTHING NEW

AS THEY LEFT YOU

YOU LEFT US TOO

OH YOU KNOW ...

JUST RUSTING WITH MY EVER MADDENING LOCKS

SECRETLY INSIDE-OUTING ODD AND STRIPY SOCKS

CATCHING SHORT BUT CLEVERLY DEEPENING SIGHS

FISHING IN WHIRLING EDDIES OF WONDER WHYS

UNRAVELLING COILS IN A SLOW AND SEEPING MELT
FECKLESS FLOW OF WORDS TO GO WILY BUT MISSPELT
UNFURLED UNDONE UNZIPPED AND TRIPPED TO FALL
CONDITIONED TO SLIDE DENIED MY SPLATTER SCRAWL

OL' MISERY

OL" MISERY"S A FRIEND O" MINE
WE OFTEN MEET FOR CHEESE „N" WINE
SOMETIMES LONELINESS COMES ALONG
WORN OUT SHOES „N" A BRAN" NEW SONG

SMOKE „N" JOKE „N" BLUFF OUR WAY
REMEMBERIN" WHEN THEM QUEENS DID STAY
FILMS „N" PHOTOS „N" BOOKS IN OUR HEADS
„N" LOVE STAINED SHEETS ON UNMADE BEDS

OUT OF SYNC

I"M WAY OUT OF SYNC

UNABLE TO THINK

MAYBE IT"S THE DRINK

THERE MUST BE A LINK

IT COULD BE YOU

IT SHOULD BE YOU

I DON'T HAVE A CLUE

NOW THAT WE"RE THROUGH

I"M WAY OUT OF SYNC

NOW THAT WE"RE THROUGH

NOW THAT WE"RE THROUGH

NOW THAT WE"RE THROUGH

I"M HERE ON THE BRINK

ALL BECAUSE OF YOU

BOOK ME IN THE CLINK

I MIGHT NEED A SHRINK

I MIGHT NEED TWO

BUT THEY"RE NOT YOU

NO THEY"RE NOT YOU

I JUST DON"T KNOW

WHY YOU HAD TO GO

AND LEAVE ME

I JUST DON"T KNOW

IT ALL SEEMS SO SLOW

NOTHING MOVES ME

NO NOTHING MOVES ME

NOW IT"S ALL FOR SHOW

THERE"S NO INNER GLOW

TO WARM ME

I WISH IT WASN"T SO

CONFUSING

I WISH IT WASN"T SO

FUCKING AMUSING

TO ALL OF YOU

OUTSIDE OUT

I"M THE LUNCH STAIN

ON YOUR PAPER

I"M THE BUTTON

OFF YOUR SHIRT

AT TIMES

I'M LIKE A GAS

INVISIBLE

AND INERT

I'M THE QUIET ONE

IN THE CORNER

I'M THE LONER

ON THE EDGE

THE OUTSIDER

AMONG OUTSIDERS

THE JUMPER

ON THE LEDGE

OWED TO LEONARD

LET''S BUILD A DREAM

AND FENCE IT IN WHITE

BUT LEAVE A FEW GAPS

TO LET THROUGH THE NIGHT

PAIR OF SHOES

IF YOU WALKED A MILE

IN ONE OF MY SHOES

AND I WALKED A MILE

IN ONE OF YOURS

I WONDER

IF WE''D FINISH UP TOGETHER

OR KNOT

PANNING FOR GOLD

ANOTHER DAY

DOWN THE MINE

AND UP AGAIN

THE HOLE GROWS

SO TOO

THE PILE OF DIRT

THE LIGHT VARIES

BUT IS

ALWAYS THERE

SOMEWHERE

I DIG

SIFT

SWEAT

HOPE

THE SPECS HIDE

SOMETIMES

THEY SHOW THEMSELVES

GLAD

TO BE FOUND

PEARL IN THE SKY

PRETTY AS A PICTURE

PEARL IN THE SKY

SHEPERDESS WITH HER FLOCK

YOU HORSE-WHIPPED ME

NOW I'M BLEEDING

ARE YOU HAPPY?

I LOVE YOU

PERFORMANCE ARTISTE

POETRY

IS A SLOW STRIPTEASE

EACH POEM

REMOVES A LAYER

GRADUALLY

WE EXPOSE OURSELVES

THE AUDIENCE

VOYEURS

THEY LOVE TO WATCH

THE MICROPHONE

SEEMS LARGER

AND FURRIER

THAN USUAL

YES ALRIGHT

IS THAT ALL YOU"VE GOT?

GET ON WITH IT

SHE THINKS

SHE SAYS

I IMAGINE WITH HER

IT"S THE SAME WITH SEX

IS THAT ALL YOU"VE GOT?

GET ON WITH IT

YOUR 2 MINUTES

ARE UP!

PINK

CHEEKS PINK

SKIN SOFT

LICK TONGUE

SWEET STICKY

LIPS DANGLE

PLEASE SIR

THE SLOW MOTION FARCE

IT HAS ME BY THE THROAT

ALL THOSE MINDLESS FORMS

CLOSED DOOR MEETINGS

ENDLESS EGO DISPLAYS

THE SILENT SOUNDS

OF CRUSHED DIGNITIES

THE HAUNTED HALLWAYS

CHANGE YOUR MIND

THERE"S A FORM FOR THAT

PRISONERS LUNATICS

THE GUARDS THE WARDENS

THE SOLD SOULS

WAITING FOR THEIR SUPER

HOPING FOR AN EASY BUY BACK

THREE MORE HOOPS

TO JUMP THROUGH

BEFORE MY DAY IS DONE

TWO MORE ATTENTIONS

TO STAND TO

BEFORE I CAN

SEE THE SUN

MAY I SKIP

TO THE LOO

MY DARLING

BEFORE I COME UNDONE

I BREATHE

MY FLEXIBLE QUOTA

ALL FULLY APPROVED

OF COURSE

PERMISSION TO GO

AND QUIETLY DIE SIR

OH YES

THREE MORE FORMS

IN TRIPLICATE

SICK LEAVE

DOCTOR"S NOTE

ANOTHER FORM

PHLEGM SAMPLE ATTACHED

MY TOILET

MY ESCAPE

MY STINKING

SHANGRILA OF PEACE

THE EXHAUST FAN

SUCKS OUT THE STENCH

I WISH IT COULD

TAKE ME TOO

POETRY COURT

YOU ARE HEREBY ACCUSED

OF CRIMES AGAINST POETRY

HOW DO YOU PLEAD?

NOT GUILTY YOU SAY?

LET US HEAR THE EVIDENCE

DID YOU OR DID YOU NOT

WILFULLY AND RECKLESSLY

ON MORE THAN ONE OCCASION

RESORT TO RHYMING COUPLETS

AND IS IT TRUE OR FALSE

THAT YOU DID KNOWINGLY

USE THAT WORD - „LOVE"

AND TRY TO DENY IF YOU WILL

THAT YOU SHOWED COMPLETE

AND UTTER DISREGARD FOR

THE LAWS OF MODERNISM

BY NEGLIGENTLY AND WITH

MALICE, FAIL TO MENTION

OR EVEN ALLUDE TO ONE

MYTH OR MYTHICAL CHARACTER

AND TO MAKE MATTERS WORSE

NOT A WHIFF OF A CANTO

NO NUMBERED STANZAS

AND YOU HAD THE AUDACITY

TO FAIL TO MITIGATE YOUR CRIMES

WITH THE SIMPLE INCLUSION

OF YOUR MIDDLE INITIAL

WHEN SIGNING YOUR NAME

BUT IT DOES NOT STOP THERE

WHERE IN YOUR, SO CALLED

POETRY, ARE THE INDIGENOUS

OR THE ICONS OF OUR LANDSCAPE

I"LL TELL YOU WHERE THEY ARE

NOWHERE! YES, THAT"S RIGHT

NOT A SKERRICK, AND FURTHERMORE

NO REDEEMING REFERENCES

TO EITHER THE GREATS OF

LITERATURE OR FOR THAT MATTER

ANY SIGN OF LIGHT HEARTED

CONDESCENSION OF OUR

BELOVED MINORITIES

IN PARTICULAR THE SEMITES

AND THE HOMOSEXUALS

GUILTY I SAY

GUILTY

GUILTY

POLARITY

DAY BECOMES NIGHT

NIGHT BECOMES DAY

DARK BECOMES LIGHT

BLUE TURNS TO GREY

GOOD BECOMES EVIL

HEAVEN BECOMES HELL

ANGEL BECOMES DEVIL

IN DARKNESS TO DWELL

SERF BECOMES LORD

GOOD GOES BAD

HAPPY GETS BORED

CHANGES TO SAD

UP GOES DOWN

IN WALKS OUT

CERTAIN OF NOTHING

ALL IN DOUBT

FIRST BECOMES LAST

OUTSIDE MOVES IN

FUTURE THE PAST

SANCTITY – SIN

BLIND REGAIN SIGHT

BROKEN MEND

BLACK TURNS WHITE

BEGINNINGS END

PROUST

BREATHE IN

BREATHE OUT

BLINK

BREATHE IN

BREATHE OUT

BLINK

BREATHE IN

BREATHE OUT

SCRATCH

BLINK

BREATHE IN

BREATHE OUT

BLINK

FART

HOLD BREATH

EXHALE

DIE

Q & A

PRISONER

NUMBER 5,000,000,051

YOUR QUESTION

ABOUT PISSING

THE ANSWER

ENJOYMENT IS ALLOWED

LIFE WOULD BE WORSE

WITHOUT IT

QUIETLY SEARCHING

I SLOWLY SEARCHED

HER VOLUMOUS SHELVES

HOPING FOR A SLOW FIX

LOOKING FOR SOMETHING

TEMPORAL BUT KNOWING

IT COULD ONLY BE

TEMPORARY AT BEST

HIGH MINDED PLANS INDEED

FOR SUCH A SPIRALLING SOUL

DIGGING ITSELF EVER DEEPER

AND YET AT TIMES LIKE THIS

THERE WAS A DISTANT GLIMMER

NOT MUCH BUT IT WAS

SOMEWHERE WAITING FOR ME

SO I THUMBED ON

THROUGH THE DUST

DARING NOT TO SNEEZE

NOR TOUCH MY EYES

FOR WANT OF REDNESS

NOR MY NERVOUS NOSE

FOR WANT OF RUNNING

I COULD NOT STOP NOW

THE HIKE HAD JUST BEGUN

AND OH WHAT SCENERY

ALONG MY MERRY WAY

ALL THE COLOURS

IN EVERY SHADE AND HUE

THE MOUNTAIN DREW ME ON

UNDER ROWS OF TREES

PAST ROCKS AND FALLS

I HEARD SOFT SOUNDS

FELT COOLNESS AND WARMTH

AT DIFFERENT TIMES

ALONG MY PRIVATE JOURNEY

AND I SAW SPECKS OF GOLD

I NOTICED OTHER STRANGERS

QUIETLY SEARCHING TOO

AND THEY MAY HAVE SEEN ME

BUT THAT WAS NOT FOR ME TO KNOW

SO I STUCK TO MY PATH

WISHING ALL THAT I COULD

STAY SAFE AND HAPPY AS WELL

I DID FIND SOMETHING

MANY TIMES OVER

AND WILL ALWAYS GO BACK

RAW

YEAH

TAKE MY BLOODIED MEAT

AND THROW IT

AGAINST THE WALL

AND HAMMER A STEAK

INTO IT

BEFORE IT FALLS

AND LOOK ON

AS IT TRIES

TO CRAWL

AWAY

AND SEE

THE SAP RUN DRY

AND WATCH IT DIE

BROWN AND GREY

WARM THEN COOL

AND HEAR IT SAY

NOTHING AT ALL

NOT A SINGLE SOUND

AND ADMIRE

THE WAY

IT GOES

QUIET AT THE END

AND SMELL DEATH

IN THE ROOM

AND WONDER WHY

THERE IS NO GLOOM

IT"S SHADES OF WHITE

AND NEVER BLACK

EXCEPT LONG AFTER

THE ATTACK

AND LOSSES COUNTED

TROPHIES MOUNTED

DARKNESS ONLY COMES

WHEN WE TURN OUT

THE LIGHT

RESPECTABLE

SHE WAS A CUTE LITTLE THING

AND SEEMED TO COME

ALL BY HERSELF

EXCEPT FOR HER MOBILE

AND THE MISSING FRIEND

SHE WAS YOUNG

BUT NOT TOO YOUNG

AND TANNED

BUT NOT TOO TANNED

SHE HAD COURAGE

ENOUGH TO COME BY HERSELF

WITH NO INTERRUPTIONS

AND NO DISTRACTIONS

THAT WAS ADMIRABLE

AND RESPECTABLE IN ITSELF

LET ALONE THOSE SHEER SHORTS

AND LEAN LEGS

TO THINK ABOUT DYING FOR

BUT NO

THE FACT THAT SHE VOLUNTEERED

AND GAVE SOMETHING OF HERSELF

FOR SEEMINGLY NOTHING

THAT WAS THE REAL REASON

FOR MY SEEDY RESPECT

AND „NO GOOD DEED ...

SHOULD GO

... UNREWARDED"

SEEING ME

SURE SHE"S UGLY

BUT SHE"S SOMEONE"S DAUGHTER

SOMEONE"S LITTLE GIRL

AND TO HER DADDY

SHE"S A PRINCESS

WE"RE ALL UGLY

IN SOME WAY

HOW WE LOOK

THE WAY WE SEE

AND IS THAT WRONG?

I DON"T KNOW

WHO MADE ME JUDGE?

OH YES ...

THAT WOULD HAVE BEEN ME

SHADOW BOXER

MY MIND DANCES

ITS OWN STEPS

OLD DANCES

IN A NEW WAY

UNREMEMBERED

BUT FELT

TO THE DEATH

THORNS IN MOUTH

AND BLOOD

SWEETER

AND DRYER

THAN WINE

I EAT LIFE

LIKE A STRANGER

AND SLEEP

THE GOOD SLEEP

OF A MAN

SATISFIED

SILLY LITTLE DREAMS

BARELY BREATHING

STAYING ALIVE

HOLDING ON

TRYING SO HARD

TO SURVIVE

SILLY LITTLE DREAMS

'SMILE HENRY'

SO I STOLE A TITLE

AND MISQUOTED IT

TO BOOT

FROM THE GREAT MAN HIMSELF

GOOGLE IF YOU WISH

YOU FUCKING PEDANTS

I COULDN'T GIVE

A CLICHÉD FLYING TOSS

MISTRUSTING

AND CUT

DULY DISCARDED

AND PASTED

COME ON YOU WANKERS

SHOOT ME

CARROT BREATH – IDIOT!

YES, THAT WOULD BE ME

YOU LUCKY BASTARDS

GETTING TIME WITH HER

YOU LUCKY LUCKY BASTARDS

CARROT BREATH – IDIOT!

GO ON

GIVE THEM SOMETHING

TO HELP DRAIN THEIR INK

A HALF EXPECTED COMMA

THEY WON'T BE HAPPY

THEN JUST SAVE IT

SOMETHING ABOUT YOU

ONE DAY I HOPE TO WRITE SOMETHING ABOUT YOU

THOUGH I DON'T KNOW EXACTLY WHAT

IT WILL DEFINITELY INVOLVE YOUR GOLD PANTS

AND THE DAY THE FAN STOPPED WORKING

AND WHEN YOU CAME OUT BACK TO TRY AND FIX IT

I ASKED IF YOU MIGHT HAVE THE MAGIC TOUCH

AND YOU SAID, "NAH I GOT NOTHIN'"

AND HOW I'LL ALWAYS LOVE THE WAY YOU SAID THAT

IT COULD BE ABOUT THE TIMES I ASKED FOR COFFEE IN MUGS

AND YOU RECOMMENDED EXTRA SHOTS

AND IT ALWAYS TASTED BETTER LIKE YOU SAID IT WOULD

OR IT MIGHT BE ABOUT THE TIME I ASKED FOR PERNOD

AND YOU SAID YOU HAD NEVER TRIED IT

SO I SAID HAVE SOME OF MINE BUT YOU DIDN'T

AND I SAID IT TASTES OF ANISEED A BIT LIKE SAMBUCCA

AND I SAID I GUESS YOU CAN'T DRINK ON DUTY

BUT YOU LAUGHED AND SAID "THAT"S NEVER A PROBLEM"

IT WILL PROBABLY INVOLVE YOUR UNIRONED SKIRT

AND OVERHEARING YOU SAY, "I"M BROKE"

AND ME FEELING BAD FOR NEVER TIPPING YOU

AND TRYING TO FIGURE OUT SOME WAY TO MAKE UP FOR IT

AND YOU BRINGING FOOD AND DRINKS OUT

AND SPILLING PARSLEY ON ME

AND YOU BENDING OVER IN FRONT OF ME

AND HOW I NOTICED YOUR BLACK UNDERWEAR

IT MAY INCLUDE ME TRYING TO FORGET ABOUT BACK INSIDE LATER

AND WONDERING IF YOU HEARD ME TALKING WITH A GUY I KNEW

AND HIM TELLING ME ABOUT THIS GIRL WHO WORKED WHERE I DID

AND HOW GREAT HE THINKS SHE IS AFTER THEY WENT SAILING

AND ME HAVING TO ADMIT I"D GONE OUT WITH HER YEARS AGO

AND THAT I WAS STILL IN LOVE WITH HER AND WONDERING

WHETHER YOU NOTICED HOW SICK I MUST HAVE LOOKED

AS MY HEART CRUMBLED WITH EVERY WORD HE SAID

I DON'T KNOW WHAT I'LL WRITE ABOUT YOU

BECAUSE I DON'T EVEN KNOW YOU

AND YOU DON'T EVEN KNOW ME

EXCEPT I MIGHT LIKE TO KNOW YOU

SO IF YOU EVER NEED A WEIRD FRIEND

I'LL MAKE MYSELF AVAILABLE AT TIMES

THEN MAYBE I CAN DO SOME JUSTICE

TO THAT GREAT WAY YOU SAY THINGS

SO REAL

AWAKE AND DREAMING

A COBWEB DANCES

IN THE BREEZE OF MY BREATH

ON A WIND OF COOL JAZZ

BLOWN BY IMMORTAL SOULS

LOST IN ETERNAL ETHER

SPIRITS SWAY IN DARKNESS

WRITHING WRAITHLIKE

WHISPERING SECRET SEDUCTION

LICKING PRISTINE FANGS

EYES ELECTRIC

CRAZY AND GONE

BLIND BUT SEEING SO MUCH

NUMB AND FEELING

EVERY SWEET RAPTUROUS NOTE

TASTING THE PUNGENT INTENSITY

OF PLEASURABLE PAIN

A RUSH SO PURE

LIKE A SPEEDING

BRAKELESS EXPRESS

HARLEQUIN HIPSTERS

TRIPPING PHANTOM LIGHTS

LUMINOUS LUNG CAVERNS

SWIRLING SMOKY SPECTRES

DRIFTING TO HEAVEN

MINDS MESMERIZED

BY MYSTIC MUSICIANS

SOFT SHIRAZ DRAPES HANG

LIKE GIANT GYPSY SKIRTS

A TIRED OLD CLOCK

KEEPS PERFECT BEAT

HEAVY LIDS SLOWLY CLOSE

CHALKY GREY ASH PAUSES

TEETERS AND FALLS

SHARDS OF GASEOUS SUNLIGHT

SILENTLY CREEP THROUGH CRACKS

GLASS SHATTERS

WITH MUFFLED SCREAMS

AND STREET NOISE STAGGERS

THROUGH A GLARING DOOR

SO SHORT

LOVELY THINGS

YEAH

WE ALL GO

SO WRITE

JUST WRITE

AND IT WILL BE

JUST RIGHT

NOT FOR CRITICS

AFRAID TO LIVE

NOT FOR PUBLISHERS

AFRAID TO PRINT

WRITE FOR YOU AND

HEARTS THAT THINK

AND PURE PAGES

THIRSTY FOR INK

FORGET ABOUT FAULTS

AND BE FREE

SHARE WITH US

HELP US FEEL

HELP US SEE

JUST WRITE

AND LET IT BE

JUST RIGHT

STICKS & STONES

HE GAZED PHARMACEUTICALLY OUT OF THE WINDOW

AT A FEW THIN STICKS LAYING ON THE GRASS

AND HE IMAGINED HER NAGGING HIM

ABOUT MOVING THEM AS SOON AS THEY FELL

RATHER THAN LATER

SO HE FOOLOSHLY SAYS

IT"S ONLY A FEW DEAD STICKS

BUT THAT WASN'T WHAT IT WAS ABOUT

AND HE WAS A NEANDERTHALL & A PHILISTINE

WHAT WOULD A CAVE DWELLING HERMIT KNOW OF THE WORLD?

STRAY CAT CAFÉ

ON A DREARY DAY TOO POOR FOR A NAME,

HE DRAGGED HIMSELF DOWN TO THE LITTLE CAFÉ,

FLAT WHITE AND A PAPER, ALWAYS THE SAME,

HE FUMBLED FOR COINS AND SOMETHING TO SAY,

HIS HAND STRUCK SILVER, BUT HIS MIND NO GOLD,

THE COFFEE MACHINE FROTHED A MOCKING HISS,

HIS SOFT FINGERS TOUCHED THE COUNTER SO COLD,

AND THERE SHE WAS, A SUNNY SHINING MISS,

ALL GLOWING WITH LIFE AND LIGHTER THAN AIR,

PINK LEMONADE CHEEKS AND STRAWBERRY LIPS,

A CHEF"S HAT HIDING HER BLONDE WISTFUL HAIR,

UNIFORM JEALOUSLY GUARDING HER HIPS,

AS SOON AS SHE SMILED, HIS FEARS DEPARTED,

AND THAT PRAISE GOD WAS HOW IT ALL STARTED.

STREET MUSIC

THE CITY"S HIS SHEET MUSIC AND LIGHTS HIS NOTES

AND AT THE END OF EVERY LINE THERE"S A BAR

WHERE RAIN PISSES RAZORBLADES ON A CAT TIN ROOF

AND HE PUNCHES DRUNK THROUGH FRESH CHILLED MIST

WITH NOTHING BUT AN OLD ROLLED BLANKET OF SHAME

STEEL WOOL BEARD RUST STAINED AND FROZEN WITH GUILT

AND HE SMELLS LIKE A CORPSE DOWN FROM THE CROSS

AND HIS HOLY MITTS SHAKE FOR NO REASON EXCEPT HABIT

AND HIS MIND WON'T REMEMBER QUESTIONS OR ANSWERS

BUT SOMEHOW HIS LIPS SHAPE WORDS WHEN NEEDED

HE KNOWS IT"S A LIE BUT THE TRUTH JUST THE SAME

CAN YOU SPARE ME A DOLLAR OR TWO?

CAN YOU MISTER ANYTHING WILL DO?

MY FRIEND LITTLE SISTER ANYTHING WILL HELP

GET ME BACK TO MY FAMILY MY WIFE AND KID

SO LONG WITHOUT ME I MISS THEM SO MUCH

SHOW ME SOME KINDNESS IN A WORLD WITHOUT JUSTICE

AND SOMEDAY SOMEWAY I WILL REWARD YOU

THANKYOU KIND SIR THANKYOU DEAR LADY

MAY ANGELS FROM HEAVEN BLESS YOU THIS DAY?

I"LL REMEMBER YOU WELL IN OUR LAST HOURS OF
JUDGEMENT

I"LL REMEMBER YOU WELL IF I"M CALLED AS A WITNESS

FOR THOUGH I MAY SEEM LIKE THE SCUM FROM THE SEWER

I"LL HAVE YOU KNOW I"M THE KING OF THE TURDS!

SWEET RAIN

THERE WAS A TIME

WHEN EVERY POEM

WAS A LOVE SONG

AND EVERY WORD

TASTED OF YOU

WHERE HANDS HELD

WARM THOUGHTS

AND FINGERS TOUCHED

AND TWIRLED

LIKE BALLERINAS

THERE WAS A TIME

WHEN YOU WERE

MY REASON

AND YOU WERE

MY RHYME

WHEN YOUR SPRING

WAS MY SEASON

AND MY WINTER

WENT ALL BUT BLIND

SUCH A TIME

FULL OF FLOWERS

FULL OF SUNSHINE

AND NEVER ENOUGH

PRECIOUS HOURS

TO BE WITH YOU

LIKE LONG HOT SHOWERS

ON ICY MORNINGS

AND STEAMY BREATHS

THAT SAY I DO

THOSE DAYS ARE GONE

TOO SOON TOO FEW

NO TUNES NO COLOURS

NO ME NO YOU

AND THOUGH MY DAYS

GROW SHORTER TOO

A DESERT GREENS

FROM YOUR SWEET RAIN

MY MEMORIES

OF YOU

SYMPTOMATIC

IT"S A WEAK DRY COUGH

AND A HEAD FULL OF CEMENT

IT"S A LITTLE BIT OF PHLEGM

EVERY NOW AND THEN

A THROAT LIKE A CHEESE GRATER

SHAVING RAW TESTICLES

A BODY LIKE SOMEONE ELSE"S

OLD SHRIVELLING SLOWLY DYING

LIKE A SLUG IN AN OVEN

ITS RED ONION EYES

WITH LEMON PEEL LIDS

IT"S THE SHORT SHARP TIP

OF A BREATH FULL OF FEAR

LIKE INHALING NEEDLES

ON EVEREST

TAPPED

HUSH ...

IT"S ONLY ME

YOUR LITTLE TAP

YOU TOUCH ME

TWIST MY KNOBS

TURN ME ON

AND OFF AGAIN

DEEP SIGH ...

DRIP, DRIP, DRIP

I RUN FOR YOU

HOT AND COLD

MOSTLY WARM

YOUR HANDS ARE SOFT

I LIKE THE LATHER

IT SMELLS NICE

DRIP, DRIP, DRIP

BUT THE OTHERS

WHO COME AND GO

AND JUST USE US

THEIR HANDS ARE HARD

THEY HURT ME

AND YOU TOO

I KNOW THEY DO

I'VE HEARD THE SOUNDS

SEEN THE BLOOD

DRIP, DRIP, DRIP

THEY SOAP AND SCRUB

BUT CAN'T WASH AWAY

THOSE SINS THAT STAIN

AND WHEN I CAN

I BURN THEM GOOD

I SCOLD THEIR SKIN

WE HATE THEM

MIRROR AND ME

SHE"S MY FRIEND TOO

JUST LIKE YOU

SHE GETS ALL MISTY

WHEN WE STEAM UP

DRIP, DRIP, DRIP

SHE TELLS ME THINGS

HOW YOU LOOK

ABOUT YOUR SMILE

THE WAY YOU CRY

AND FROWN AT TIMES

YOUR HAIR PLAYS TRICKS

AND WHEN YOU LAUGH

WE DO TOO - WITH YOU

SO MUCH SOMETIMES

MY WASHERS JUMP

AND MIRROR SHIMMERS

AND YOU BOTH VIBRATE

WE LOVE YOU FRIEND

DRIP, DRIP, DRIP

TEENAGE GIRLS

ALL DOLLED UP

PEROXIDE AND GLOW

PERMANENT POUTS

RED LIPSTICK

SMEARED SO THICK

LIKE PARIS PRO"S

SKIRTS CHECKED AND PLEATED

HIGHER THAN THE EIFFEL TOWER

CHAUFFEURED TO TRAIN STATIONS

BY SPOILING PARENTS

OFF TO FIND BAD BOYS

AND BE LEERED AT

BY GOOD BOYS

AND OLD MEN

TEXTING GIRLFRIENDS

INCESSANTLY

LIKE NERVOUS HABITS

TEN PAST FOUR

THE SCREECHING OF THE SAW

THE LEECHING OF THE WHORE

SHORT-LIVED VOWS WE SWORE

OUR HOLY HEARTS WE TORE

LIFE"S SIMPLE JOY NO MORE

PLAYING DRESS-UPS IN THE STORE

THE WARMING WOOL WE WORE

WATCHING SHIPS FROM SHORE

THE CLOUDS WITHIN THAT POUR

THE NEVER HEALING SORE

THE CONSTANT SEARCH FOR MORE

THOSE RULES THAT BREAK THE LAW

THE NEVER BEING SURE

NOT KNOWING WHAT LIFE"S FOR

NOW OR THEN OR NEVERMORE

THE TIME WAS TEN PAST FOUR

THAT RABBIT

THE AUGUST LIGHT

BURNED LIKE ACID

A FOOL TWIDDLED

HIS LEGS SHOOK

SHE LOOKED HAPPY

ON THAT BIG DARK SCREEN

LIKE A GIANT LOVERS LANE

WITHIN HIS MIND

AND SHE WAS

HIS STAR OF EVERYTHING

AND HE WAS

HER DYING SERPENT

AND SHE REMAINED

AMAZINGLY CUTE

YOU KNOW

LIKE A RABBIT

OH HE"D DIG FOR HER

AND THEN

HE COULD

FINALLY REST

THE CLOSER YOU GET

HAVE YOU EVER BEEN SO AFRAID?

YOU JUST FELT LIKE RUNNING

SO FAR AWAY

NO-ONE COULD FIND YOU

BUT YOU WERE SO AFRAID

YOU COULDN"T TAKE ONE STEP

AND THEN

BY THE TIME YOU DID

YOU WERE FURTHER

THAN YOU EVER DREAMED

AND YOU COULD SEE

SO CLEARLY

ALL YOU NEEDED

WAS TO GO BACK

THE COLD OLD FOREST

SNOWFLAKES SOFTLY FALLING, FALLING

WIND AND WOLVES CALLING, CALLING

PINE TREES POINTING SOARING, SOARING

BROWN BEARS SNOOZING SNORING, SNORING

FIELD MICE SCURRY HIDING, HIDING

WILD CAT CHASING SLIDING, SLIDING

FAT MOON SMILING BEAMING, BEAMING

WINTER"S BREATH STEAMING, STEAMING

THE CUTEST THING

SHE IS JUST THE CUTEST THING,

SHE IS MY AUTUMN AND MY SPRING.

LIKE A LOTUS, OPEN, CLOSE,

WAKE AND DANCE, TIRE AND DOZE,

WAY TOO SMART, I LIKE HER MIND,

SHE"S HEAVENLY BUT HARD TO FIND.

FUNNY GIRL, SHE MAKES ME SMILE,

KEEPS ME WAITING QUITE A WHILE,

SOMETIMES SHY, SOMETIMES COOL,

I"LL BE PATIENT, BE HER FOOL.

SHE IS JUST THE CUTEST THING,

SHE IS MY AUTUMN AND MY SPRING.

THE LADY AND ME

WE MET LONG AGO

IN A PREVIOUS LIFE

THE LADY AND ME

WHEN SHE WAS A CAT

AND I WAS A FLEA

I WAS HER ITCH

AND SHE WAS MY SCRATCH

THE LADY AND ME

WHEN SHE WAS A CAT

AND I WAS A FLEA

SOMETIMES SHE"D LET ME

SLEEP IN HER FUR

SO SOFT A BED

THE TICK OF HER HEART

THE LICK OF HER PURR

SOMETIMES SHE"D LET ME

DRINK FROM HER MILK

FROM HER SPECIAL DISH

ME JUST A PEST

WITH HER WRAPPED IN SILK

WE WERE SO HAPPY

SUCH AN ODD PAIR

A FAT LITTLE FLEA

AND HIS FELINE QUEEN

HER TAIL IN THE AIR

THOSE WERE THE DAYS
IN THAT PREVIOUS LIFE
THE LADY AND ME
I LIVED LIKE A KING
LIKE SHE WAS MY WIFE

NOW I'M LONG GONE
FOR I WAS A FLEA
AND SHE LIVED ON
FOR SHE WAS A CAT
QUITE UNLIKE ME

SOMETIMES I WONDER
IF SHE CAN SEE
IN HER DREAMS
WHEN SHE SCRATCHES
HER FAT LITTLE FLEA

SO LONG AGO

IN THAT PREVIOUS LIFE

THE LADY AND ME

WHEN SHE WAS MY CAT

AND I WAS HER FLEA

THE LETTER

AND YES I SMELLED THE PAPER

OF THE LETTER THAT YOU WROTE ME

IT STARTED WITH A SAYING

THAT AT FIRST I COULDN"T FOLLOW

BUT THEN I UNDERSTOOD

OR THOUGHT I DID

AND IT WAS YOU

GIVING PART OF YOU TO ME

AND EVERY PART IS SACRED

VULNERABLE AND TRUE

I LOVE BEAUTY AND

THAT"S ALL I SEE IN YOU

THE PRINCESS AND THE LUNE

I CREEP IN

AND LINGER

AWKWARDLY

IN THE DOORWAY

AND EVENTUALLY

SIT BETWEEN

KURT AND LOVER BOY

AND MY MEAL FOR THREE

COMES WITH BEER

AND FRIES

AND SALAD

AND I EAT

AND OFFER

AND SHARE

AND KURT EATS

AND LOVER BOY DOESN'T

AND THE PRINCESS

IS TALL AND THIN

SMART AS HELL

BUT HATES MEN

AND DREAMS

IMPOSSIBLY

OF RESPECT

FOR HER MIND

SO BEAUTIFUL

AND KURT SAYS

ISN"T SHE GREAT?

AND I SAY NOTHING

BUT THINK

I"D RATHER LOOK

AT HER

THAN LISTEN

TO ALL THAT FEMINIST CRAP

AND MY EGO

SINKS BACK INTO ITS HOLE

AND I CLAP

WITH GOOD MANNERS

THE ENLIGHTENED

WITH THE MAD

AND THE WAITRESS

EXUDES LIFE

LIKE I REMEMBER

FROM YEARS AGO

AND MY MIND

WANTS TO TIP HER

AND MY GROIN

WANTS TO WHIP HER

AND KURT FINISHES OUR MEAL

AND LOVER BOY FEIGNS DISDAIN

AND I CLAP ON

LIKE A PRIEST

IN AN ORGY

OF NUNS

THE RIVER & THE SUN

SHE IS FROM AND OF WATER

HER THOUGHTS ARE A STREAM

WHEN SHE IS FILLED

SHE REACHES OUT AND TOUCHES

SHE DIVIDES AND CONQUERS

SHE IS THE WATER OF CLEOPATRA

OLD AS THE DAWN

FRESH AS YOUTH DEW

SHE FLOWS LIKE A MELODY

SATURATING THE SENSES

AND SHE GIVES EVERYTHING

DOWN TO HER LAST DROP

AND HER LORD LOVES HER

FOR ALL THAT SHE IS

HER GRACEFUL BEAUTY

HER MAGIC SPARKLE

EVEN HER BROODING DARKNESS

THE WAY SHE BATHES IN HERSELF

CALMLY REFLECTING HIS GOLDEN GAZE

SHE IS AWARE OF HIS POWERS

YET SHOWS NOT A RIPPLE

SHE IS COOL AS THE NIGHT

BUT TOUCHED BY HIS WARMTH

FEELING IT GENTLY FLOW THROUGH HER

AND WHEN SHE STRETCHES

LAYING NAKED BEFORE HIM

HER SKIN SHIMMERS

AND HER DEPTHS DAZZLE

HER JEWELS ARE BLINDING

AND HE IS A LUSTFUL KING

HE WOULD HAVE HER ONLY FOR HIM

SHE IS FLATTERED AND SEDUCED

BY HIS MAJESTIC DEVOTION

AND HIS EYE ONLY FOR HER

AS HE SLOWLY TAKES HER

SHE KNOWS HIS DESIRE

SHE STIRS AND SURGES

HE LIFTS HER LIKE A MISTY VEIL

AND CARRIES HIS VIRGIN BRIDE

ACROSS HIS REAPING THRESHOLD

AND SHE ANOINTS HIM

WITH EXQUISITE PERFUMED OILS

AND SHE IS PURELY SPENT

HE IS HUMBLED BY HER

AND THEY ARE A DREAM

WHEN THEY WAKE

HE IS A THIEF

AND SHE IS WISER

THE ROMANCE OF WOLVES

I'LL MISS IT

I'LL MISS THE THRILL

THE CHASE

THE RACE

BEFORE THE KILL

I'LL MISS IT ALL

THE NATURAL CALL

THE PANTING

BREATHLESSNESS

AND SO MANY DREAMS

UNFULFILLED

THE SLOW BURN

THE LITTLE CANDLE

BURNS ON

NIGHT AFTER NIGHT

KNOWING ITS FATE

NOT COMPLAINING

JUST BEING

THE ODD SIZZLE

OLD FRIEND

THE AIR

SUDDENLY TURNS

AND INVISIBLY

BECOMES

EXECUTIONER

THE WIND

NEVER GIVES IN

NOT MUCH

BUT ENOUGH

FOR US

TO SHARE

THE CANDLE

LIVES

DIES

ONCE

A HUNDRED TIMES

THE BURN

ALWAYS DOWN

THE WAX

MELTS ON

TO REST

SHORT AND FAT

THE FLAME

ALWAYS UP

OR SO IT SEEMS

THE STAINS

HER STAINS

HAVE BECOME MINE

AND I NEEDED THEM

LIKE I NEEDED HER

NOT TO KEEP HER

BUT TO REMEMBER

THE STAINS

AND KNOW

HOW IT FEELS

THE TAMING OF THE BEAST

OH I LOVE YOU DEARLY MISS

THOUGH YOU FRUSTRATE ME SO

I AM FULL OF FAITH IN YOU

AS THOUGHTS GO TO AND FRO

I SO OLD AND YOU SO YOUNG

WHO"D HAVE THOUGHT IT TWICE?

THAT FIRE COULD LEARN PATIENCE

FROM MELTING BLOCKS OF ICE

AND THOUGH I PULL AND STRUGGLE

AS YOU RUN ME ROUND THE RING

NOW I KNOW YOU MEAN NO HARM

ONLY PRAISE FOR YOU I SING

AND WHEN I FEEL THE STING OF WHIP

AND BITS BETWEEN MY TEETH

I"LL UNDERSTAND IN YOUR FIRM HAND

LOVE LOOMS IN VEINS BENEATH

YOU WILL TAME THIS BRUTISH BEAST

AND SO GRATEFUL WILL HE BE

WHEN YOU RIDE UPON HIS BACK

SUCH WONDERS BOTH SHALL SEE

THE VERY LAST

I'LL GIVE YOU ALL

BUT MY VERY LAST

I'LL KEEP THAT

JUST FOR ME

AND THEM

ALL THOSE ONES

PARTS OF TWOS

AND THREES

OF LOVE

THE MULTIPLIER

YOU DESERVE ALL

EXCEPT THAT

MY VERY LAST

TOO MUCH BURDEN

FOR ANYONE

THE WILD-WILD WEST

EVERY DAY"S A GOLD RUSH

AND YOU CAN"T TRUST NO-ONE

COZ THEY"RE ALL DOUBLE-NEGATIVES

AND HANGING"S A SPECTATOR SPORT

AND WRITING"S FOR TOMBSTONES

AND REAL MEN DOWN WHISKEY

AND EVERYONE"S YOUR FRIEND

AND ITS DRINKS ALL ROUND

THE GUNSLINGER"S IN THE BELLTOWER

AND WOMEN HIKE UP THEIR SKIRTS

AND WEAR BOOTS OVER FISHNETS

BUT IT"S NOT LIKE THE MOVIES

WHERE THE SHERIFFS AREN"T CROOKED

AND THE VILLAINS ALL DON BLACK

AND EVERYONE"S YOUR FRIEND

AND ITS DRINKS ALL ROUND

IT"S A DRY ARGUMENT IN A DUSTBOWL

AND YOU CAN'T TAKE A BATH

COZ THE TOWN"S GOT NO WATER

SO YOU WASH ONCE A MONTH

WITH A JUG AND A BASIN

AND THE BEDBUGS DON"T MIND

AND EVERYONE"S YOUR FRIEND

AND ITS DRINKS ALL ROUND

THE PREACHER"S DAUGHTER"S NO VIRGIN

LUCKY YOUR HORSE KNOWS THE WAY

COZ YOU"RE A WRECK IN A DESERT

AND THE FLOWERS ARE ALL CACTUS

AND YOUR HAT"S FULL OF HOLES

FROM ALL THOSE NEAR MISSES

AND EVERYONE"S YOUR FRIEND

AND ITS DRINKS ALL ROUND

YEAH EVERYONE"S YOUR FRIEND

AND ITS DRINKS ALL ROUND

THIS DAY

I"LL USE

WHAT I HAVE

FIRST

HATING TO IMPOSE

CHLORINE

IN THE NOSE

ONE MORE LAP

AND IT STICKS

LONG AFTER

THE ROSE

HAS SHOWN

HERSELF

WITH PENCIL SKIRT

ALL SET TO BLOOM

FOR TEASING WIND

AND SUMMER DRIPS

ON LOSING THREADS

EXQUISITELY

TRAGIC

A SMOOTH SHUFFLE

OF SLOW MOTION

CRUSH

LUSTING FOREVER

LIKE LIQUID SUN

TO ALL

OH

HOW THE MIGHTY FALL

AND FALL

AND FALL

AND DAVID

LAYS ON CLAY

BUT RAISES

TO THE SUN

A GOLDEN CUP

FOR ALL

FOR ALL

A CRY RINGS OUT

A SERMON CALL

NO BELLS

NO TEMPLE

PEACE

TO ALL

TO A POETESS

I WONDER IF YOUR WORDS ARE FREE

AND IF MY INNER EYE MIGHT SEE

CLIMBING UP YOUR FRUIT FILLED TREE

A THORNY DEVIL MUCH LIKE ME

TOAST-MASTERS

HERE"S TO THE POWER ELITE

THE GODFATHERS

AND GODMOTHERS OF POETRY

HERE"S TO THE EDITORS

THE ARBITERS OF TASTE

WHO MAKE AND BREAK POETS

HERE"S TO THE HAND-WRINGERS

THE PSYCHOLOGICAL CASTRATORS

THE NETWORKERS AND CRONIES

HERE"S TO THE SYCOPHANTS

THE SUCK HOLES AND SELL-OUTS

ALL THE HANGERS ON

HERE"S TO THE PUBLISHERS

THE POLITICALLY CORRECT

AND ALL THE TRIPE THEY PRINT

HERE"S TO THE PRETENDERS

THE DEAD JOURNALS

AND THE BENEFITS OF HINDSIGHT

HERE"S TO THE FARCICAL WASTE

ALL THOSE BORING BOOKS

THE ONES REAL PEOPLE DON"T READ

HERE"S TO THE OTHERS

THE REJECTED

THE UNPUBLISHED

THE UNFASHIONABLE

THE UNCOMPROMISING

THE UNAFFECTED

THE DISCONNECTED

THE DISENFRANCHISED

THE INDEPENDENTS

THE INCORRUPTIBLE

THE ANARCHISTS

THE HERETICS

THE LONERS

THE QUESTIONERS

THE SEEKERS OF TRUTH

THE DOWN AND OUT

THE POWERLESS

THE MEEK

THE STRONG

THE THICK SKINNED

THE ONES WHO NEVER GIVE UP!

TO JOSEPHINE

HOME IN FOUR DAYS

MY CRÈME CARAMEL

DON'T BATHE CHÉRI

MY OYSTER NATURÉL

TOO MANY QUESTIONS

HOW MANY HOURS IN A LIFETIME?

HOW MANY THOUGHTS TO GO MAD?

HOW MANY DRINKS MAKE A DRUNKARD?

HOW MANY WHORES HAVE BEEN HAD?

HOW MANY DROPS IN AN OCEAN?

HOW MANY LINES IN THE SAND?

HOW MANY STONES IN A MOUNTAIN?

HOW MANY BOYS MAKE A MAN?

HOW MANY SPOTS MAKE A LEOPARD?

HOW MANY CLOUDS MAKE A STORM?

HOW MANY LIES MAKE A FARCE?

HOW MANY DEATHS WILL WE MOURN?

HOW MANY BUGS IN A VIRUS?

HOW MANY TOLLS IN A BELL?

HOW MANY DEVILS IN HEAVEN?

HOW MANY ANGELS IN HELL?

HOW MANY SINS MAKE A SINNER?

HOW MANY SOULS WILL WE SELL?

TWO UNCONNECTED THINGS

IT"S ABOUT YOU, AND IT"S ABOUT ME

TWO UNCONNECTED THINGS

I"M OVER YOU, AND I"M A LIAR

SO WHY DO I STILL, THINK ABOUT YOU EVERY DAY?

AND WISH YOU"D COME, AND STAY

OR GO FOREVER, AND JUST SAY NEVER

IT WAS SO NICE THE WAY, WHEN WE WERE APART

EACH DAY, WE"D LOOK FOR EACH OTHER, IN THE USUAL
PLACES

AND REMEMBER, THE FUNNY THINGS ABOUT OUR FACES

AND IT WILL NEVER, BE THE SAME

AND I JUST CAN"T, SPEAK YOUR NAME, AGAIN

BECAUSE IT HURTS TOO MUCH, AND I MISS YOUR TOUCH

AND I ALWAYS WILL

NO MATTER HOW MUCH, I TRY TO FORGET YOU

AND I"LL NEVER EVER, GET OVER YOU

BUT WHAT DO I KNOW?

I"M JUST A FOOL, WHO THINKS TOO MUCH?

AND FEELS TOO MUCH, AND GETS THINGS WRONG

TOO MANY TIMES, SO MANY TIMES

I'VE JUST LOST TRACK, AND WANT YOU BACK

BUT KNOW YOU"RE GONE, FOR GOOD THIS TIME

AND WON'T COME BACK, AND NEVER WILL

AND IT"S MY FAULT AND YOUR FAULT TOO

AND YOU"RE STILL GONE, AND THERE"S NO WAY BACK

AND YOU"LL MOVE ON, AND I"LL PRETEND

AND YOU WILL MEND, AND I"LL PRETEND

IT"S NOT THE END

I"M OVER YOU, AND I"M SUCH A LIAR.

TWO WAY MIRROR

OH UGLINESS

THIS MASK

THAT GROWS UPON ME

WITH AGE

DEAR FRIEND

SUCH A GIFT YOU GIVE

THE VIRTUOUS VISION

OF THE SAGE

TO SEE THE TRUTH

THE CURSE THOUGH

IS IT SEES YOU TOO

UNWANTED

SUNDAY CAME AS AN UNCLE

HE'D BEEN AWAY

DOING TIME

BROUGHT WITH HIM A PRESENT

WRAPPED IN CARDBOARD

TIED WITH STRING

TO HIM IT MEANT EVERYTHING

TO YOU IT WAS NOTHING

US

ONCE THERE WAS JUST US

THE LITTLE MISS AND I

THEN ALONG CAME YOU

AND IT WAS US

INCLUDING YOU

THEN YOU LEFT

AND IT WAS JUST ME

AND LITTLE MISS AGAIN

I AM ME

AND YOU ARE YOU

AND SHE IS SHE

AND WE ARE AS WE ARE

AND AS WE THINK

WE"RE MEANT TO BE

VARIETALS

I LIKE ALL KINDS

OF FLOWERS

FROM FRESH LITTLE DAISIES

TO THORNY OLD ROSES

THE YOUNG ONES

AND THEIR SWEET

HONEY DEW

THE OLD ONES

WITH THEIR MUSK

AND LAVENDER BLUE

BUT DAB IN THE MIDDLE

GLOW MY NEMESEEDS

THOSE EDGY WILD VIOLETS

SO MUCH LIKE YOU

WANTED

SO WHAT DO YOU WANT?

I JUST WANT SOMEONE WHO LOVES ME

OH IS THAT ALL?

WELL THEY NEED TO REALLY LOVE ME

THAT"S BETTER

IT NEEDS TO BE A BIT DIFFICULT

WATER FINDS ITS WAY

JUST AS A RIVER MUST FLOW FROM HIGH TO LOW

LIFE"S JOURNEY IS MUCH THE SAME

AND THO WE GROW FROM SMALL TO TALL

THE PATH IS THE SECRET TO THE GAME

WHEN ALL IS DONE AND WICKED WISDOM SHOWS

TRUE HAPPINESS KNOWS NOT HIGHS OR LOWS

FOR PURE JOY IS MERRY AND JUST CONTENT TO BE

AND THIS IS ALL THAT TIME WHO TAKES SO MUCH

BUT IN RETURN WOULD HAVE YOU KNOW

AND AS A FINAL GIFT GIVE UNTO THEE

WEIRDOS

WE SAT TOGETHER

IN THE CROWD

LOOKING AND LISTENING

TO THE FOOL WHO WAS A GENIUS

THERE WAS AN EMPTY SEAT NEXT TO US

AND A HAIRY MAN CAME AND SAT

HE SMELLED LIKE WET DOG

BUT HAD A CAMERA AND TOOK PHOTOS

THEN HE LEFT AND WE WERE ALONE AGAIN

IN THE CROWD

AND THE FOOL WHO WAS A GENIUS PLAYED ON

UNTIL HIS WIFE SAID STOP

IT WAS LATE AND TIME FOR BED

WHAT IS LEFT UNSAID

WE CAREFULLY SPEAK

AROUND THE PAINFUL LOSS

AS THOUGH THE WORDS

FORM A DISTINCT OUTLINE

OF WHAT IS GONE

LIKE A GRAPHIC PHOTO NEGATIVE

THE BACKGROUND DEFINES THE IMAGE

THE DARKNESS FOCUSES THE LIGHT

THE BLACKNESS SURROUNDS THE WHITE

OUT OF RESPECT

WE AVOID MENTION

OF THE DEAD

WHO KNOWS?

I LOVED HER ONCE

BUT THAT WAS LONG AGO

SHE LOVED ME TOO

HOW MUCH I"LL NEVER KNOW

I LOVE HER STILL

BUT HAD TO LET HER GO

I ALWAYS WILL

HOW MUCH SHE"LL NEVER KNOW

WORLD AT WAR

I

THE WORLD IS AT WAR

IT HAS ALWAYS BEEN THAT WAY

AND IT WILL ALWAYS BE THAT WAY

SINCE LIFE BEGAN

THERE HAS BEEN A STRUGGLE

TO EXIST AND SURVIVE

WE ARE ALL AT WAR

BACTERIA, FUNGI, INSECTS,

ANIMALS, HUMANS, VIRUSES,

GRASSES, FLOWERS, TREES

THE EARTH AND OTHER PLANETS

THE STARS AND THE MOONS

THE OCEANS AND THE RIVERS

ALL AT WAR

THE BATTLES RAGE EVERY DAY

THERE ARE MOMENTS OF PEACE

WHERE WOUNDS ARE TREATED

AND THE DEAD REMOVED

WE PAUSE AND REFLECT

BUT EVEN THEN WE FIGHT

WE FIGHT BACK TEARS

WE COMPARE SCARS

WE CANNOT FORGET

ALL THOSE WARS

FROM THE PAST

WE PLAN NEW WARS

AND DREAM OF NEW BATTLES

WITH BIGGER AND BETTER WEAPONS

WE THINK ABOUT HOW MUCH STRONGER WE ARE

AND SOME PITY THE WEAK

SOME LOOK WITHIN

AND FIND MORE WAR

PAST, PRESENT, FUTURE

ALL AT WAR

PARENTS WITH CHILDREN

PARENTS WITH PARENTS

CHILDREN WITH CHILDREN

FAMILIES AGAINST FAMILIES

GENERATIONS AGAINST GENERATIONS

RICH AGAINST POOR

LOW AGAINST MIDDLE

MIDDLE AGAINST UPPER

LOW AGAINST LOW

HIGH AGAINST HIGH

ALL WANTING MORE

ALL AT WAR

II

BIG BUSINESS AGAINST SMALL

BIG AGAINST BIG

SMALL AGAINST SMALL

ALL AGAINST ALL

THE EVERY DAY STRUGGLE

FOR MONEY AND GOLD

OIL AND SHARES

FOR HOUSES AND CARS

SHIPS AND PLANES

TANKS AND GUNS

STATUS AND POWER

THE ECONOMIC WAR

THE STRATEGIC WAR

THE INTELLIGENCE WAR

THERE"S AN OXYMORON

SPY AGENCIES AT WAR

AID AGENCIES AT WAR

ARMIES AT WAR

NOT ONLY WITH OTHER ARMIES

BUT ALSO WITH THEMSELVES

ARMIES WITH NAVIES

AND AIR FORCES

AND SPECIAL FORCES

FIGHTING WITHIN

FOR FUNDING AND POWER

OFFICERS WITH TROOPS

GENERALS WITH GENERALS

GENERALS WITH POLITICIANS

POLITICIANS WITH POLITICIANS

VOTERS AGAINST VOTERS

ALL FIGHTING FOR POWER

BOSSES WITH WORKERS

FARMERS WITH BANKS

AND LOCAL GOVERNMENTS

AGAINST STATE

AGAINST FEDERAL

PARTIES AGAINST INDEPENDENTS

UPPER HOUSES WITH LOWER HOUSES

UPSTAIRS AGAINST DOWNSTAIRS

NEIGHBOURS AGAINST NEIGHBOURS

MEN AGAINST WOMEN

MEN AGAINST MEN

WOMEN AGAINST WOMEN

AGAINST TRANSSEXUALS

AND HOMOSEXUALS

AND BISEXUALS

AND PAEDOPHILES

PRISONERS AGAINST PRISONERS

AGAINST WARDENS

LAWYERS AGAINST LAWYERS

BARRISTERS AND SOLICITORS

JUDGES AGAINST JUDGES

BLUE COLLAR AGAINST WHITE

RACE AGAINST RACE

REDNECKS AGAINST BLUEBLOODS

BOATPEOPLE AND TOURISTS

ALL AT WAR

III

NIGHT AND DAY

STRUGGLING FOR TERRITORY

OVER LAND AND BORDERS

PROFITS AND TAXES

WATER AND VIEWS

AND LOCATIONS

AND PARKING SPACES

AND RAGING IN TRAFFIC

JOSTLING FOR POSITIONS

AND RACING TO WIN

TO GET THERE FIRST

THE RAISE

THE PROMOTION

THE NEW CAR

THE NEW SUIT

THE NEW SHOES

THE BIGGER OFFICE

THE TRAVEL

THE ALLOWANCES

THE TICKETS TO THE GAME

TO WATCH THEM ALL FIGHTING

SCREAMING AND YELLING

TO GET THE BEST SEATS

OR THE CORPORATE BOX

AND GOD HELP ANYONE

THAT GETS IN THE WAY

OF THE SPECTACLE IN THE ARENA

THE WAR TO WATCH THE WAR

AMONG THE PLAYERS

AMONG THE SUPPORTERS

AND THE COACHES

AND THE SPONSORS

NOT MUCH HAS CHANGED

IN THOUSANDS OF YEARS

SINCE THE ANCIENT GREEKS

AND ROMANS

AND ALL THE OTHERS

THE GLADIATORS

AND THE SLAVES

AND THE KINGS

AND THE EMPERORS

AND THE KNIGHTS

AND THE PEASANTS

AND THE LADIES

AND THE SERVANTS

ALL AT WAR

IN ONE WAY OR ANOTHER

IV

EVEN THE CLERGY

THE PRIESTS AND THE HIGH PRIESTS

THE BISHOPS WHO WOULD BE CARDINALS

AND THE CARDINALS WHO WOULD BE POPES

THE RELIGIOUS WHO PREACH PEACE AND LOVE

YET PRACTICE HATE AND INTOLERANCE

AND GO TO WAR

IN THE NAME OF GOD

THOSE UNHOLY CRUSADES

RELIGION AGAINST RELIGION

CATHOLICS AGAINST ANGLICANS

AGAINST MUSLIMS

AGAINST HINDUS

AND HERETICS

AND WITCH HUNTS

BY ELDERS AND STATESMEN

POETS AGAINST POETS

MUSICIANS AGAINST MUSICIANS

PAINTERS AGAINST CRAFTSMEN

SKILLED AGAINST UNSKILLED

THE INTELLECTUALS

AND THE FOOLS

OFTEN ONE AND THE SAME

THE FAT AND THE THIN

THE TALL AND THE SHORT

THE HIPPIES AND THE ZEALOTS

THE SPIRITUALISTS

AND ATHEISTS

AND AGNOSTICS

THE QUIET AND THE LOUD

THE ROMANTICS

AND THE GROUCHES

THE BEAUTIFUL

AND THE UGLY

THOSE WHO CARE

AND THOSE WHO DON'T

THE INDIGENOUS

AND THE IMMIGRANTS

THE CITY DWELLERS

AND THE COUNTRY FOLK

THE TALKERS

AND THE LISTENERS

THE WRITERS

AND THE READERS

ALL AT WAR

WITH THEMSELVES

AND WITH OTHERS

V

THE FAMOUS WHO SEEK PRIVACY

THE NOBODIES WHO WANT TO BE SOMEONE

THE VOICELESS WHO WANT TO BE HEARD

THE SICK WHO WANT TO BE CURED

THE LOVELESS WHO WANT TO BE LOVED

THE UNPOPULAR WHO WANT TO BE POPULAR

THE OLD WHO WANT TO BE YOUNG

THE YOUNG WHO WANT TO BE OLDER

THE MEEK THAT LACK SELF-ESTEEM

THE DAMAGED

THE BROKEN

THE TORN

ALL THE CASUALTIES OF WAR

THE CONSTANT NEVER-ENDING

RELENTLESS MESS OF WAR

THE TIRING DEGRADING

MENTAL AND PHYSICAL BATTLE

AND IT WILL NEVER END

THE NEWBORN REPLACE THE DEAD

AND WHO KNOWS IF DEATH BRINGS PEACE

EVEN DEATH ITSELF MAY JUST BE YET ANOTHER STRUGGLE

LIKE THE JOURNEY FROM WAKE TO SLEEP AND DREAMS

AND NIGHTMARES

AND WAKE AGAIN

EVEN THEN THERE ARE MORE WARS

FEARS AND JOYS

AND BATTLES TO FIGHT

MOUNTAINS TO CONQUER

FLIGHTS AND FALLS

LIFE IS STRANGE

AND UNEXPLAINABLE

AND MEANING SUBJECTIVE

ALL I KNOW OR AT LEAST THINK IS

THE ESSENCE FOR ME IS SURVIVAL

AND THAT IS A CONSTANT BATTLE

www.ingramcontent.com/pod-product-compliance
Lightning Source LLC
Chambersburg PA
CBHW052000090426
42741CB00008B/1477